FATE, FORTUNE & MYSTICISM
IN THE
PERUVIAN AMAZON

FATE, FORTUNE & MYSTICISM
IN THE
PERUVIAN
AMAZON

---

*The Septrionic Order
and the
Naipes Cards*

MARLENE DOBKIN DE RIOS, PH.D.

Park Street Press
Rochester, Vermont • Toronto, Canada

Park Street Press
One Park Street
Rochester, Vermont 05767
www.ParkStPress.com

Text paper is SFI certified

Park Street Press is a division of Inner Traditions International

Library of Congress Cataloging-in-Publication Data

Dobkin de Rios, Marlene.
  Fate, fortune, and mysticism in the Peruvian Amazon : the Septrionic Order and
the naipes cards / Marlene Dobkin de Rios.
     p. cm.
  Includes bibliographical references and index.
  ISBN 978-1-59477-372-3 (pbk.)
  1. Fortune-telling by cards—Peru. 2. Sacred Mystical Order of Septrionism.
3. Fate and fatalism. I. Title.
  BF1878.D63 2011
  299'.93—dc22
                                                                            2010039886

Printed and bound in the United States by Lake Book Manufacturing
The text paper is SFI certified. The Sustainable Forestry Initiative® program
promotes sustainable forest management.

10   9   8   7   6   5   4   3   2   1

Text design and layout by Virginia Scott Bowman
This book was typeset in Garamond Premiere Pro with Trajan Pro, Caslon, Legacy
Sans, and Myriad as display typefaces

To send correspondence to the author of this book, mail a first-class letter to the
author c/o Inner Traditions • Bear & Company, One Park Street, Rochester, VT
05767, and we will forward the communication.

CONTENTS

PART TWO

Destiny and Personal Control

Septrionic Concepts in Mysticism

INTRODUCTION

Fortune-Telling Cards, Mystical Reflection in Peru

Men at sometimes are masters of their fates:
The fault, dear Brutus, is not in our stars,
But in ourselves, that we are underlings.

JULIUS CAESAR, ACT I, SCENE II,
WILLIAM SHAKESPEARE

This is a book about destiny. This is a book about fate and fortune. This is a book about poverty in the Peruvian Amazon. This is a book about the Sacred Mystical Order of Septrionism in Peru, a spiritualist philosophy that has views about the management of our destiny. At some level, Cassius's remarks in *Julius Caesar* (quoted above) apply to the actions of the river's-edge farmers living in an Amazonian shantytown, which I studied as an anthropology graduate student in 1968–1969, given that these words are particularly focused on the concept of *underling*, meaning "dependent." During that year, I became a fortuneteller, using a deck of cards called *naipes*, which had a long history of hundreds of years of use. The cards originated in China and were carried to India by Hindustanti-speaking Gypsies. Eventually, they found their way to Europe—as early as the thirteenth century—and were probably brought to Central and South America for gaming by priests during the fifteenth-century Conquest.

My career as fortune-teller took place in that very poor urban shantytown, where I learned to read these cards according to a system supposedly developed by an eighteenth-century adept, Madame Marie LeNormand, advisor to Napoleon and his empress, Josephine. Applying this technique, which was already present in the culture, to the poverty-stricken peasants in Iquitos, Peru, I drew on my anthropological, sociological, and psychological training to find hidden structures within the cards in order to explain my successes in reading the naipes for large numbers of people there. Subsequently, I joined the Sacred Mystical Order of Septrionism, a Peruvian spiritualist philosophy and religion, and learned a totally different approach to managing our destiny—not, as some men in Cassius's time did, by throwing the future onto the stars or blaming ourselves and our tendency for dependence, or in the case of the Beleños, through the predictions of the naipes. Rather, the spiritualist doctrines of self-control and the incorporation of Septrionic mystical beliefs in dealing with our destiny provide a major departure from the underling, dependency philosophy inherent in fortune-telling.

This book chronicles the development from belief in fortune-telling naipes to Septrionic beliefs in self-control and provides the reader with a full understanding of what is actually involved in the successful reading of fortune-telling cards in the Peruvian milieu. It also speaks to us with insights gleaned from a study of Septrionic doctrine.

Certainly, when anthropologists participate in the life of another society, they are often absorbed into the local realities. Another form of life penetrates their consciousness. What anthropologists call *participant observation* leads them to inhabit their informants' religious worlds, despite warnings from the academy that we must maintain our distance and avoid bias by maintaining separation from the "other." Yet extraordinary experiences often result from in-depth participation in those aspects of local culture considered most meaningful by members of the society being studied, and provide data that cannot be obtained any other way.[1]

Anthropologists must share a level of reality with their informants that outsiders do not normally have available to them. Perceptions become altered. Some, like myself, try to apply a rational grid to aid in understanding what is actually going on. As we will see, this yields some very interesting data on just how these urban farmers casting their fate on the stars can lead to specific prediction "hits" that appear to have a truth of their own. Often the anthropologist participating in some aspect of the informant's behavior may share the intense involvement of native participants.

Though all societies have some technique of forecasting the future, the Westerner typically doesn't believe that we can truly foresee it. Little is gained by debating the truth-value of a technique such as the naipes, but the structure of prediction can be very helpful to our understanding of the outcomes. Are there multiple realities at work, multiple ways of experiencing the world?

As Young and Goulet argue, since the 1990s, anthropologists began to take experiential rather than rational approaches to extraordinary experiences. In my work with the fortune-telling cards, I do both, and in part 1 of this text, I share my insights. Then, in part 2, we turn to the Septrionic doctrines about destiny and its management by individuals, and we find that in linking mysticism and science, we are provided with a special way to examine these phenomena.

Chapter 1 focuses on the fortune-telling cards and their history and structure. The images of the naipes themselves (see insert) and their meanings will be laid out for you to see in chapter 2, should you desire to learn to read the cards yourselves. I gained insights as a practicing *curiosa,* or reader of the cards, in Belen, an urban Amazonian shanty-town in Iquitos, Peru. In chapter 3, we turn to the so-called culture of poverty in Belen to understand what propels the Beleño to pay the anthropologist/fortune-teller to read his fate. Chapter 4 allows us to see just how magic works from the inside—because, as any graduate student would, I kept careful notes—with regard to the particular predictions and the actual fulfillment of those prophecies.

To provide an alternative to attributing our fate to the stars, in part 2, you will read about the Sacred Mystical Order of Septrionism, which I joined in 1977. This order provides specific spiritualist doctrines that propose a particular explanation for the kinds of poverty we see in Belen, and a different doctrine and concept of destiny and its management to guide its members.

At the end of the text, a glossary helps to define foreign words that occur throughout the book.

Let's turn now to the naipes and begin our journey.

PART ONE

Destiny, Fate, Fortune, and Poverty

Reading the Naipes

1
THE HISTORY AND
THE STRUCTURE
OF THE NAIPES

The naipes are used often by folk healers who cure with herbs or psychedelic plants in a society in which witchcraft beliefs exist and people often expect that illness is caused by the evil will of others. The cards become a psychological adjunct to a healer's therapy, a sort of intake procedure to learn more about a client so that the healer can appear to be omnipotent and replete with knowledge and power. We cannot talk about the naipes as a divination technique without understanding the context in which these cards are used, particularly among the urban poor of Belen, who live in abject poverty in their shantytown. Healers are able to manipulate situations of misfortune that dog the steps of the urban poor as the healers diagnose illness and misfortune, appearing all-powerful and worthy of their fees.

I first ran into the naipes in Peru when, as a graduate student, I was sent by the Institute of Social Psychiatry at San Marcos University on the north coast of Peru to a special village, Salas, an hour and a half outside of Chiclayo. It was said that there more than a hundred folk healers used, in healing rituals, the San Pedro cactus laden with mescaline. Attending a healing ceremony one night in Salas, I heard a folk healer tell his wife to bring the naipes down to the area where the patients were seated. Having a long-term interest in fortune-telling, I asked the healer to tell me more about the naipes. He brushed me off, but this sparked my interest, which had been dormant for a number of years. When I arrived in Peru, I was game for divination techniques. In the marketplace in the nearby city of Chiclayo, an hour away from Salas, I purchased a pamphlet said to be written by Napoleon's spiritual adviser, Madame LeNormand, as well as other leaflets without attribution of an author. Available in the bibliography are a number of books and pamphlets that offer advice across the ages in telling fortunes with the naipes. In chapter 2, I provide the designations Napoleon's advisor gave to each of the cards, which I used during the year I spent in Peru. Some of the other pamphlets were said to be Italian, French, or Spanish in origin.

Madame LeNormand was born in a small village in France in 1773 and arrived in Paris when she was twenty-one years old. She opened a

Figure 1.1. Naipes from the colonial period in Peru (before 1821)

salon and read the fortunes of a number of highly placed individuals who were politically active in the French Revolution, including Robespierre. Apparently, Josephine de Beauharnais, later married to Napoleon Bonaparte, was one of her clients, and Madame Marie was reputed to have regularly read the naipes for Napoleon.

Most of the booklets based on her system agree on basic principles. Certain days of the week are most propitious for a reading—Friday, Saturday, Tuesday, and Wednesday, for example. The client must cut the cards only with the left hand, which is nearest to the heart, or else the fortune obtained is thought not to be accurate. The person who takes it upon himself to read the cards must be sincere and strong and not frivolous. This card reader should also be observant and wash his hands and face before using the cards. Dropping a card while reading a fortune is said to bring bad luck. The system provided by Madame LeNormand was reprinted in four additional booklets. It is not the actual content of the system that is important to analyze. If we can get to the heart of the divining cards by using a rational mathematical probability statistic and examine the technique in light of what I have called an "ethno-projective device,"[1] we can learn a good deal about traditional folk psychotherapy.

The naipes help healers to tap in to the causality of illness while, at the same time, allowing them to present themselves as all-powerful. This cannot help but dispel fear, anxiety, and self-doubts in their patients and provide a high expectation of cure. This personal influence of healers increases their manipulation of the patients' anxieties and provides a path toward eventual cure.

In addition to studying the basic principles, we will also look at intuition and pattern recognition as further explanations for success in reading the naipes.

WITCHCRAFT BELIEFS AND ILLNESS

The residents of Belen recognize and openly discuss illness they believe to be caused by the malice of others. This becomes important in understanding the motivation of Beleños to seek out their fortune and often to discover who has caused them to be bewitched. Informants speak of malice everywhere—for instance, the evil will of neighbors and relatives who frequently seek out a witch to cause harm. Healers who use the hallucinogenic plant ayahuasca receive visits from patients who not only want to be healed from an illness but also may want to bewitch someone in particular for purposes of revenge. Some *curanderos* reject the proposition to do evil, but others specialize in the use of these hallucinogens for that purpose—the *brujo* (witch) is socially shunned and secretive. Many ayahuasca healers themselves read the naipes at an initial interview of a client who is readying to take the hallucinogenic purge. This is done in order to get an idea of the stress facing the client. Again and again, I observed men and women talking out loud during a reading, exclaiming that such and such a misfortune would be laid at the feet of a mother-in-law, an envious neighbor, and the like, making it easy to see just what stresses were present in that person's interpersonal environment.

Regarding witches, this class of individuals was known to harm others. Unlike African societies, in which witchcraft was suspected but never proved, in the Amazon, these witches are ready to take hard cash in advance to harm a client's enemy. They keep a little book in which they write down the details of the psychic "hit." Listed below are the main illnesses suffered by the Beleños, which often propelled them to seek help, first by a *curioso,* who reads the naipes, and subsequently by an ayahuasca healer to reverse the magical spell and return it to the perpetrator.

Susto

This illness is found throughout Peru and Latin America and includes many cases of a profound alteration of metabolism or nervous disorders. It originates in a violent impression of fear. Many people believe that *susto* has a supernatural origin, which is produced when a person's soul magically separates from the body.

Daño

This is an illness that is believed to be due to a witchcraft hex. *Daño* has various symptoms and chronic development. It can be caused by motives of vengeance or envy. In the Amazon, it is believed that daño is caused by a powerful medicine thrown on the threshold of a house in the early hours of the dawn. It can cause a period of bad luck, called *saladera*. Witches use ayahuasca, the plant hallucinogen, to cause this illness. The *ayahuasquero* claims to fly through the air and cause incurable illnesses and horrible misfortunes to his client's enemies. Some believe that witches control a series of spirits, whom they call upon to cause the evil. Still others believe that a thorn can be sent through the air, like a lance, toward an enemy. The witch is paid in advance on behalf of the vengeful client.

Pulsario

This illness is marked by symptoms of anxiety, hyperactivity, and inquietude without precise causes. In general, it attacks women. Sometimes it is experienced as a tumor localized in the mouth of the stomach. It is a hard mass that can cause pain, anguish, or anger that cannot be expressed.

Despecho

This is the rancor that a person feels toward another, which can provide the necessary motivation to seek out a witch. Like daño, various bodily pains are attributed to the malice of one person against another.

Mal de Ojo

This syndrome is found throughout the Peruvian Amazon and all of Latin America, and is known in English as the *evil eye*. It includes symptoms of nausea, vomiting, diarrhea, fevers, weight loss, insomnia, and depression. It is motivated by envy and afflicts children and adults whose personal beauty has caused them to be victims of the evil eye. Beleños believe that their neighbors or relatives envy whatever good fortune they may have. Anything can attract envy—a light-skinned complexion, appearance of good health, indications that a person is eating well, and so forth. A person can provoke the malice of others if he has an amorous spouse or if his house is free from rancor. The naipes reading functions as a diagnostic tool as much for the client as for the ayahuasquero. Clearly, the client has his suspicions, but the answer to one of the three questions posed by the client toward the end of the reading generally confirms his suspicions as to the cause of an illness. In Western medicine, we expect an answer to the questions "How did my body break down?" "What are the mechanisms?" "What medicine/technology must I engage in order to get better?" In Peru, there is a different focus among the urban poor. The questions they ask include, "Why am I ill, as opposed to someone else?" "Who is the perpetrator who has caused my body to break down in one way or another?" "Why me?" Any diagnostic tool such as the naipes reading or an ayahuasca session can be called upon. The role of the ayahuasca healer is to return the evil to the perpetrator before beginning to treat the illness. This explains the haste with which people want their fortunes told: Tell me now, right now!

HISTORICAL DATA ON THE NAIPES

Printed playing cards have been traced by Alfred Kroeber, one of the important founders of anthropology, to tenth-century China, and they appear four centuries later, almost simultaneously, in several European countries such as Italy, France, Germany, and Spain. Kroeber suggested that either the Mongols or the Muslims might have transmitted such cards from China to Christian nations, despite the fact that Islam forbids all gambling. Another theory, mentioned already, is that Hindustani-speaking Gypsies, according to Papus and Levi, brought the cards from India to Europe. A game of French playing cards called tarot, used in divination and popular during the Middle Ages, was believed to have resulted from an adaptation of a card game called *naibi* (also referred to as *nayb* and known in Italy in the fourteenth century), to which was added a series of point cards. There are many theories about the origin of the naipes, some linking the cards to the minor arcana of the tarot[2] or the esoteric Jewish kabbalah traditions. In the naipes deck, there are three picture cards in each of four suites: the King, the Caballo (Horse), and the Sota (Page). The Pages are used to represent women, and the Caballo and King represent men with different traits and characteristics. The Jack in Western card decks is replaced by the Sota (Page). The twenty-two major tarot cards are said to be related to the letters of the Hebrew alphabet.

If we turn to the dictionary of the Royal Spanish Academy, the term *naipes* is etymologically derived from the Arab word *naib*, "he who represents," or *laib*, "he who plays." Mention of the cards occurs in the thirteenth and fourteenth centuries and may have been introduced into Europe by the Crusaders. The game of naipes was said to symbolize the feudal structure of society. By 1377, the naipes were in wide use. The Gypsies were the first to use the cards for divination. If playing cards used in divination were known in fourteenth-century Spain, it would not be at all difficult, despite the lack of historical documentation, to trace the movement of such divinatory aids to Spanish America. Certainly, the Conquest period was a time in which men seeking adventure and wealth in unknown lands might be expected to take gaming cards along with them. A deck of forty or forty-eight cards, small and easily portable, without doubt found its way into the Hispanic world at the time of the sixteenth-century Conquest. On a trip to Argentina in 1968, I was fortunate to visit the National History Museum in Buenos Aires, where I held in my palm a very early deck of naipes, hand painted on parchment material, small enough to fit into someone's pocket or baggage.

A famous historian of Peru with Spanish and Incan heritage, Garcilaso de la Vega, published a drawing that shows abuses practiced by members of the clergy who gamed at cards. Still in the realm of speculation, we can only surmise that these cards became absorbed into Peruvian folk-healing practices. Today these cards are used throughout Latin America, not only for fortune-telling but also for entertainment and gambling.

FOLK MEDICINE AND THE NAIPES

Folk healers such as those in Peru treat many psychosomatic disorders. Native healers are most effective when there are psychosomatic and other psychological components to illness that have been precipitated by social complications. Such folk healers may be in a position to be more effective if their training and judgment from past experience predispose them toward a higher expectation of emotionally and culturally precipitated illness. Native healers have prestige, and they offer reassurance and suggestions to their patients. Any divinatory technique such as that of the naipes can tap in to culturally induced stresses, which contribute to illness. A healer who utilizes a technique such as the naipes can remove from the sick person agency and responsibility for a decision and cast it upon the heavens. If the healer is able to manipulate the divinatory technique in a clever manner, he can understand the source of the disorder, which can be part of conflict-filled and anxiety-laden social relations. In chapter 3, we look in more detail at Belen and the culture of poverty at the time of the study.

What is clear is that the naipes are not simple amusement for the clients but rather are used by them and healers as a diagnostic technique, especially when most clients believe that illness is caused by evil willing or witchcraft machinations on the part of "others." The healers manipulate a category that I call misfortune cards to plumb the depths of interpersonal conflicts, material loss, and sickness or death of loved ones to make their diagnosis.

READING THE NAIPES

To read the naipes, the cards are laid out on a flat surface in the form of a cross, called St. Andrés. A picture card representing the client— called the interested party—is placed in the center of the cross, and a frame is made of cards, which encloses the picture card representing the interested party. The frame consists of three additional cards placed on the left side of the client's picture card, three below this picture card, three on the right side, and three above the client's central picture card. Beneath the card representing the interested party is an extra card, which the client doesn't see until the very end of the reading. This card is deemed to shed light on some aspect of the reading.

The total number of cards read is eighteen. The client (the interested party) is, as said, represented as a figure card in the center of the cross. The top three cards predict the future. Effectively, this type of reading permits a large number of possibilities for each reading and four major story lines for each part of the reading. As mentioned, placed beneath the interested party is the additional card that the client doesn't see until the end of the reading, representing someone or some element important to the story line.

THE STRUCTURE OF THE NAIPES

For images of the naipes cards, see the insert. Six cards of the total corpus can be classified as signifying outright misfortune:

Ace of espadas (spades)	pain, perfidy, envy, jealousy
Two of bastos (clubs)	sickness, death, pain, affliction
Three of copas (hearts)	embarrassment, hurdle, insecurity, delay
Four of espadas (spades)	jealousy, bad intention, trap, lasting suffering
Five of espadas (spades)	hidden sadness, anxieties, disgust
Seven of espadas (spades)	long suffering, immense pain, terrible agony

In addition, another eleven cards, when occurring upside down, also signify general misfortune:

Ace of oro (diamonds)

Ace of bastos (clubs)

Ace of copas (hearts)

Two of oro (diamonds)

Two of espadas (spades)

Two of copas (hearts)

Three of oro (diamonds)

Three of bastos (clubs)

Five of bastos (clubs)

In reading the cards, there is a random pattern. The deck is first mixed and then cut by the client. The reader chooses a series of cards placed in a particular patterned arrangement mentioned above—the cross of St. Andrés (see figure 1.2 on page 16). I followed this system in which only a partial selection of the cards is made—18—out of the total corpus; thus the client is choosing his destiny. By cutting the deck this also signifies to the client that free will is exercised by his choice of the cards. Thus, only some of the cards in the deck are read in the cross of St. Andrés, and the rest are set aside until three questions are asked at the end of the reading, when all the cards in the desk are mixed and cut again.

Flexibility is the key in reading the cards in order to phrase meaningful utterances from the discrete elements that constitute the drawing. This depends on the skill of the reader. A story is told from the sequence of three to four cards, which are read as a single unit around the interested party in the center of the cross. Twelve of the cards in the naipes deck refer to people—men and women of various physical attributes. Throughout the reading, the client is the interested party assumed to be directly connected to the meaning obtained from the cards. After the reading is completed, the client may ask three questions, and each question permits a yes or no answer. The curioso turns alternate cards face up. If the Ace of oro appears, the answer to a question is affirmative. The number of cards

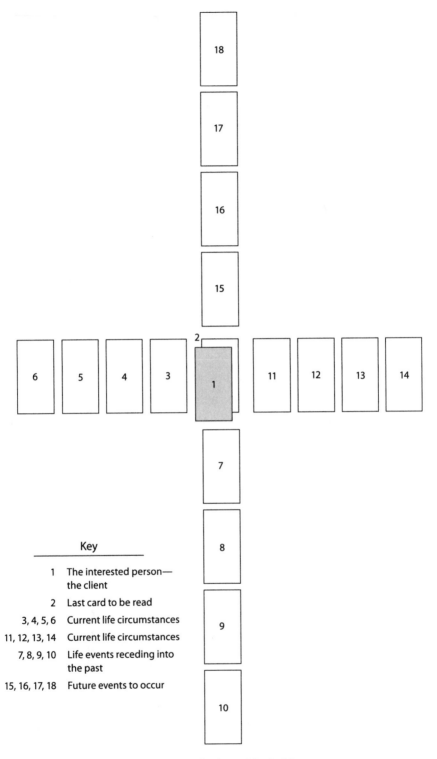

Figure 1.2. The Cross of St. Andrés

read before the Ace of oro appears indicates a time line; for example: seven days, seven weeks, seven months until the prediction will be realized.

A probability statistical analysis of the naipes indicates that in an average reading of eighteen cards, the probability that at least one misfortune card occurs is 99.76 chances out of 100.[3] Two misfortune cards will occur at a probability of 97.40 chances in 100. For three misfortune cards to appear, the statistic drops to 87.3 chances in 100. By the time we reach four misfortune cards, we are close to a 50 percent probability. Because each misfortune card is modified by preceding and sequential cards, an interpreter is in a position to construct a story line quite possibly focusing on interpersonal conflict, material loss, or illness. Thus, the deck is loaded not in the direction of good fortune but rather to highlight stress and conflict that may be present in the sociocultural milieu. I have called this fortune's malice, from a line in the poem "De Gustibus" by Robert Browning.

A healer, faced with a patient who suffers from psychosomatic illness, could easily give a reading and expect to tap some source of conflict, stress, or anxiety in the patient's life. The manner and skill of the reader or healer in telling his tale and presenting the omnipotent knowledge he derives from the cards is a very clever information-gathering technique. Healers will not allow outsiders to be present at the readings, nor will they discuss their techniques, because they feel that such a skill justifies a monetary compensation and should not be divulged freely. This would explain the proliferation of inexpensive paperback primers that are easily available in the marketplace.

THE NAIPES AS AN ETHNO-PROJECTIVE DEVICE

The naipes looked to me, a medical anthropologist, to be an ethno-projective device comparable to Western psychotherapeutic techniques of free association, dream analysis, and projection. We see this in psychological tests such as the Thematic Apperception Test (TAT) and the Rorschach. Though Western tests have been translated and used in other cultures since the 1930s, little if anything has been done to utilize measurement devices that are already present in a given cultural environment. The naipes allow the anthropologist a first-rate opportunity to tap areas of projection—the world of private and personal meanings held by the individual and the social group.

The cards should be viewed as part of the cultural complex—a series of neutral stimuli whose symbols and meanings are shared by both the healer and his patients in a world laden with misfortune, illness, suffering, and despair. Chapter 3 details much of this culture of poverty and the effects of modernization on the Amazon cultures.

The cards can be manipulated in a random manner to yield a pattern of fantasy and a particular association of ideas that fit within a worldview that focuses on the origin of illness due to magical activity such as witchcraft. The cards present the patient with neutral, ambiguous stimuli. This allows the card reader to see how internal perceptions and feelings are replaced by external perceptions. Classic projection is an unconscious and pathological process in which an individual defends against unacceptable impulses or qualities in himself by inaccurately ascribing them to individuals in his outer world. Generalized projection is different. It is a normal process in which an individual's inner states influence his perception or interpretation of the world. The naipes are used by both the healer and the patient in this world of magical causality of disease perhaps corresponding to classic projection. The world of the client in terms of interpersonal relations is fraught with envy, fear, despair, anxiety, and the like. Yet the naipes have a good deal in common with dream analysis, word association, and Western-derived psychological tests by permitting the scientist entry into the individual's private world. In chapter 3, we examine in some detail the parameters of life in a Peruvian slum and how this influences the readings of the naipes. Of great interest to me was the way in which each client whose fortunes I read "talked" along with the reading of the cards as the story line progressed, identifying evildoers as particular enemies or rivals, or family members with whom they didn't get along. This permitted the card reader to make better sense of the themes that followed, and at times, the curiosa could modify the reading to reflect the new information that was forthcoming.

THEMES IN THE NAIPES COMPARED TO THOSE OF WESTERN PSYCHOLOGICAL TESTS

Anthropologists over the decades have given Western psychological tests, translated into native languages, to the people they study. These include the Rorschach and the Thematic Apperception Test, which tap in to the personality traits of their informants. Themes often emerge from these studies to help the anthropologist better understand the people she is studying. These tests, however, are often useless when worldviews from one culture are imposed upon another. We must find other ways to learn about a culture without projecting our own devices such as these tests onto members of that culture.

For me, the naipes were what I called an ethno-test for healers, which developed in Peru over a four-hundred-year period. The system enjoyed uncounted prior use, arriving in Peru with the Spanish Conquest in the early sixteenth century. As mentioned, priests probably brought the naipes with them. The cards were small and portable for gaming, and they became integrated in divinatory techniques by enterprising individuals. These ethno-tests can be learned and administered by anthropologists to tap in to thematic materials present in the society they are studying. Most of the psychological tests focus on pathology, namely psychological illness. It is easy to label people neurotic or psychotic, but life events can be stressful, and the desire to forecast the future appears to be a human universal. The psychological tests often represent Euro-American goals, motivations, and expectations. With the administration of Western-based psychological tests, it is difficult to establish rapport between the tester and the client. The naipes, on the other hand, are familiar in the culture, and they are presented to informants in a meaningful way, which they understand. Moreover, through a monetary charge for their use, it is acknowledged that the naipes have currency in the community.

WESTERN THEMES VERSUS NAIPES THEMES

When I left California to conduct my year's fieldwork in Belen, a colleague of mine in the psychology department of the University of California, Los Angeles, gave me the Thematic Apperception Test to take along. I was able to work with a sample of forty-five women to whom I gave the TAT while the naipes were logged in with another sample of forty-two women. There are some real differences in the responses of the clients to these two instruments. I knew all the informants, at least casually, and I had conversed with them on a variety of topics prior to the testing. When I read the naipes to my clients, the responses were spontaneous and positive. The TAT, however, which consists of a number of photographic-like ambiguous pictures, asked the clients to state what they saw, indicating to them that different people see different things. This testing caused obvious distress to many of my visitors. They often said, "I don't know," or "How should one know?" or "How can I tell?" I had to cajole and urge the women to take the TAT, and the respondents typically demonstrated embarrassment.

These major themes emerged:

1. Generalized sadness, with many different TAT cards eliciting responses although no reasons were given
2. Illness and death themes, which appeared very frequently
3. Happiness, particularly when the response was that the woman was in the presence of relatives or was going to meet them

4. The eliciting by one TAT card of many responses of demons and folkloric characters, including horrendous happenings

5. The emergence of some religious imagery, such as the Virgin Mary and various saints, who were identified by individual TAT cards

6. A focus on travel, often to get to work

With the readings of the naipes, on the other hand, I soon realized that a number of themes were repetitive and that the technique could be used to gather meaningful thematic data. Those individuals whose cards I read could be said to be a random sample, although skewed toward those who were open to knowing their future by means of a divinatory technique. Because each individual could ask three questions of the cards, I could abstract recurrent themes:

1. Great fear of abandonment by the spouse and particular distrust by women of being left to raise their children without economic support

2. Distrust characterizing relations between men and women

3. Desire to travel to new areas of the region or to Lima to obtain work and achieve job security

4. Desire for economic security and wealth

5. Amorous escapades plotted and divined

While the cards were being read, additional remarks spontaneously emerged. These included great distrust of neighbors and relatives, lack of self-confidence, adultery temptations and activities, intimate sexual confidences, interpersonal strife and conflict, honest/dishonest behavior with loved ones, desire for children, and fear of sickness. Misfortune cards, discussed earlier, which deal with long suffering, terrible misfortune, obstacles, and the like, were often interpreted by the clients in the readings to apply to particular individuals in the figure cards. Important "others" in the client's world emerged, and general category cards such as money cards, happiness cards, love thoughts, ill usage, debts, reconciliation with loved ones, and so on could be woven into general stories whose purposes and details were left vague. While my readings always had a vagueness about them so that clients could make sense of them in terms of their own life experiences, they did weave themselves into general stories, which served to stimulate and trigger confidences that I could not obtain in the six months of fieldwork that I had completed, despite my adequate language skills in Spanish and reasonable rapport with the Beleños.

COMPARISONS

Figure 1.3 shows thematic difference in terms of percentages of total responses between the two samples of women that occurred when I used both tests among the Beleños. Each test tapped into different themes, although there is slight overlap. The naipes very definitely tapped in to life concerns when compared to the TAT. The TAT is set up for a psychologically infirmed audience; it reaches into affective areas and taps into depression, anxiety, and trauma. The naipes, on the other hand, in addition to focusing on existential life problems and individual psychological preoccupations, resulted in fewer negative responses. The cards never seemed strange to my clients, nor did they cause stress, discomfort, or total rejection. In fact, my role as a fortune-teller was valued, and I was sometimes woken up at the break of dawn to predict the future of someone who was ready to set off for Lima. Clearly, my use of the fortune-telling cards brought forth a complementary set of themes and cultural materials when compared to the TAT. Moreover, I was able to establish a culturally acceptable role for myself and was able to gather interesting and important data on the community.

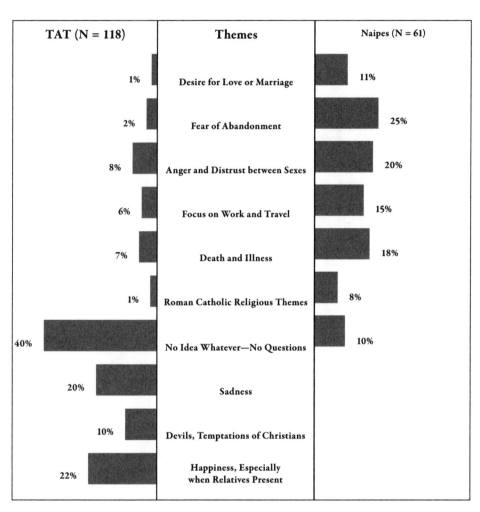

Figure 1.3. Comparison of themes between TAT and naipes
(by percent of total responses)

THE NAIPES

Images and Meanings

Listed here are the cards in the forty-card Spanish naipes deck. (See color plates in the insert for images of the cards, presented in the order in which they're listed here.) Also included here are the meanings attached to each card, which I used during my fieldwork in Belen. These are derived from pamphlets available for sale in the Chiclayo Peruvian marketplace, which are said to be provided by Madame Le Normand, the spiritual adviser to Napoleon, among others. Each reading places at the center of the cards one picture card, which represents the client. If the client is a female, the Sota, or Page, is placed to correspond to the interested party. If the client is a man, one of the Caballos or Kings is selected, according to the client's skin coloring—for example, light skin or dark skin—or other characteristics, such as being in the military, being kind and generous, and so forth. We shouldn't forget that the Moors, who came from the Middle East and North Africa, were dark complexioned and resided in Spain for more than eight hundred years, influencing symbolic systems such as the naipes.

There are four suits: copas (hearts); oro (diamonds); bastos (clubs) and espadas (spades). (I use the English terms for the common playing deck). The fortune-telling deck that I used in Peru consisted of forty cards comprising seven number cards and three figure cards in each of four suits. This is called the Spanish deck (*barraja española*). An exhibit on games held at the Lowie Museum of Anthropology at the University of California, Berkeley, in 1976 included medieval tarot cards. The caption stated that the four suits of medieval European cards originally represented four classes of society. Spades were the nobility, hearts were the clergy, diamonds were the merchants, and clubs were the peasant farmers.

The Naipes Card	Card Meaning
Ace of copas	marriage, passion, love, joy, pleasure, sweetness, intoxication, delight, religious retreat, friendliness
Ace of oro	good fate, sure money, good luck, happiness, joy, richness, opportune hour, justice, health, delight, pleasure
Ace of bastos	firmness, loss of control, amorous subject (affair), ill usage, good harvest, power, worldly wealth, glory
Ace of espadas	pain, perfidy, envy, jealousy, sentiment, passion, bad tongue, calumny (gossip), disgust
Two of copas	love thoughts, good intentions, maternal tenderness, love of spouse, love security
Two of oro	acquittance in a lawsuit, collection of debts, interest, paper money, avarice, business, riches
Two of bastos	cradle, sickness, death, pain, affliction, sadness, funeral, danger, trap
Two of espadas	letter, news, knowledge of certain people, encounter, arrival, voyage, written magazine, motive, book, augury
Three of copas	embarrassment, hindrance, obstacle, bother, hurdle, interruption, insecurity, defect, delay, stupefaction
Three of oro	good fate, happiness achieved, accomplished success, certain happiness, assured gain, good business, entire satisfaction

The Naipes Card	Card Meaning
Three of bastos	friendship, marriage, union, agreement, reconciliation, kinship, brother, wife, reunion, ties with others
Three of espadas	justification, justice, good sentence, rectitude, occasional perfidy and pain
Four of copas	amorous triumph, love security, love intention, words of love, thoughts of love
Four of oro	business, determination, negotiation, intention, affectation, business proposition, injunction
Four of bastos	end, seal, duty, firmness, constancy, security, end of suffering, opportunity, masculine honor
Four of espadas	hard, difficult, jealousy, bad intentions, cruelty, bitter, lasting suffering, war, honor in war, trap, wounds by steel
Five of copas	baptism, meal or supper, good life, invitation, wedding, inn, provisions (food), occasional love thoughts
Five of oro	gain, good success, good business, good luck
Five of bastos	road, collection of debts, steps, inquiry, desire to obtain news, on the road, through the road
Five of espadas	imaginary suffering, hidden sadness, anxieties, disgust
Six of copas	excessive tenderness, grand passion, indomitable love, firmness in love, without control, amorous fury, durable
Six of oro	recovery of debts, good augury, satisfaction in money, lawyer
Six of bastos	voyage, embarkation, locomotion, car, push off, wind, fierce pursuit
Six of espadas	without thinking, soon, at the moment, occasional pain and disgust from news received

Ace of copas

Ace of oro

Ace of espadas

Ace of bastos

Two of copas

Two of oro

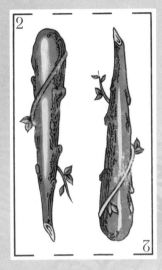

Two of bastos

Two of espadas

Three of copas

Three of oro

Three of bastos

Three of espadas

Four of oro

Four of copas

Four of bastos

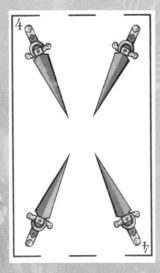

Four of espadas

Five of copas

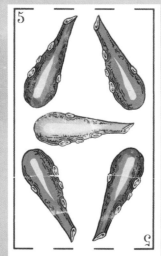

Five of bastos

Five of oro

Five of espadas

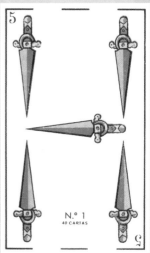

Six of copas

Six of oro

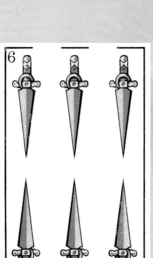

Six of bastos

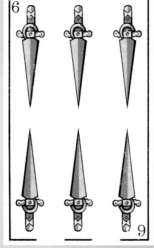

Six of espadas

Seven of copas

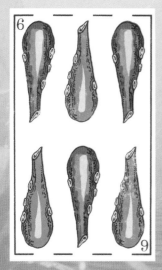

Seven of oro

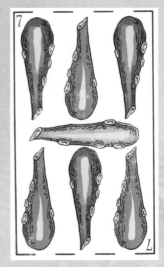

Seven of bastos

Sota of copas

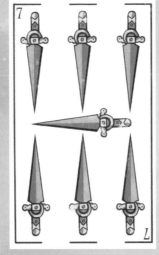

Seven of espadas

Sota of oro

Sota of bastos

Sota of espadas

Caballo of copas

Caballo of bastos

Caballo of oro

Caballo of espadas

Rey of copas

Rey of bastos

Rey of oro

Rey of espadas

The Naipes Card	Card Meaning
Seven of copas	at the gate, preparation for good, good disposition, sure effects
Seven of oro	lottery, game, drawing, move, surprise, prepare yourself for luck, get ready for good or bad luck
Seven of bastos	agriculture, harvest, wheat, bread, profit, plantation, flowers, branches
Seven of espadas	future, time, long-suffering, terrible misfortune, immense pain, terrible agony
Sota of copas	woman of good color, happy
Sota of oro	rich or blond woman
Sota of bastos	virtuous brunette woman
Sota of espadas	woman firm in love, jealous
Caballo of copas	wastrel, gay dog (male), undertakes many projects
Caballo of oro	absent rich man
Caballo of bastos	brunette male traveler
Caballo of espadas	absent military person
Rey of copas	man of good color, wastrel, given to love
Rey of oro	blond, rich resplendent man
Rey of bastos	brunette man, firm and generous
Rey of espadas	man of good color, military

The cards cited here correspond to an English deck of common playing cards, which theoretically could be altered to adhere to the Spanish deck. This alteration would require removing the eights, nines, and tens to conform to the only forty cards per reading that are used in Peru. Jacks, Queens, and Kings are represented in a different order than the official Spanish deck. The Jack (called a Page, or Sota in the Spanish translation), numbering one in each of the four suits, is used to designate a woman. The Queen in the common English playing deck is actually a male of particular characteristics: the Caballo (or Horse). The King is the same in both the common playing card deck and the Spanish deck. Interestingly, there are eight cards representing men and only four cards representing women, which is probably indicative of the fact that more women than men seek out their fortunes from the cards, placing their faith in a destiny that they don't control and expressing their dependence upon men in their lives.

Let's turn now to Belen and the culture of poverty to see how this culture influences fortune-telling.

3
BELEN

The Culture of Poverty, the Naipes, and Love Magic

To understand the place of the naipes in controlling our destiny, it is important to know something about the men and women who seek out the curiosos to read their fortune—and pay for the service despite the dire poverty in which they find themselves.

The rainforest region of Peru, particularly the northwest Amazon, is an area of the world that Western civilization has influenced for more than four centuries. When the European explorers and missionaries came to this area of the Amazon, they found river's-edge tribal Indians practicing horticulture as a way of life. As the result of the heritage of the Conquest, two distinct groups emerged. The first were the nonliterate Indians who exploited the tropical rainforest habitat through fishing and horticulture. The second group developed as the result of intermarriage between the Europeans and Native American peoples, giving rise to the individual with dual heritage: European and Native American. In most of Latin America the term to define those with this dual heritage is *mestizo*. Among the offspring of Europeans born in Latin America is the *criollo,* which we will discuss shortly. We can add to these influences those of Western civilization inculcated through mass media, the movies, newspapers, radio/TV, the army, schools, libraries, hospitals, the Internet, and so on.

As the result of this mixture of Indians and mestizos, a third category emerged particularly after World War II, when large numbers of mestizo-izing *cholos* left their river's-edge homes in distant provinces and migrated to large cities such as Iquitos and Pucallpa to seek better educational and economic opportunities for their children. Cholos as a group emanated from the lowest stratum of society. Historians believe the term may date back from the colonial period and was a derogatory Spanish synonym for "dog." To some, this term represents a relatively well-to-do Indian who seeks the status of mestizo but has not yet "arrived." The cholo is not an Indian in the eyes of the Indians, nor is he a mestizo in the eyes of a mestizo. It is, in fact, an elastic category that describes a great variety of people who occupy a marginal setting between traditional men and women and mestizos. Although the cholo's social origins are similar to those of the Indians, his income and occupational independence relate him more to the mestizo. Subtle racial markers distinguish one group from another. These are gradients of skin color, facial form, hair type, and surnames. In these local classifications, lifestyles in particular are the most important markers.

Belen, as an urban shantytown, serves as a port of entry for thousands of jungle migrants who undergo a process of becoming cholos. This was the case in 1968–1969, when my fieldwork was completed, and continues to be so today. Some segments of mestizo culture dismiss the cholo's love magic and traditional healing with plant hallucinogens (including ayahuasca) and label it as superstition. This is especially so among devout Catholics and extends particularly to customs of magical behavior in consulting the naipes and using hallucinogenic drugs such as ayahuasca. Such beliefs, however, persist with great tenacity despite the efforts of the dominant society to suppress them. To further complicate the mix, there is the concept of criollo culture. This is a set of distinct patterns of culture and behavior that are associated with Spaniards and with Lima, and particularly with Lima's urban middle class. The term

Figure 3.1. Scenes of Belen

originally referred to offspring of Europeans who were born in Peru. The values of the criollo include the phenomena of avoidance of hard work and placement of a high value on cunning and liveliness, and preferences for definite kinds of diet and music.

The cholo is a marginal person in that his self-identity is new and insecure. Such a person is highly mobile geographically and occupationally. Generally, he speaks Spanish in addition to another Indian language. He does, however, stand out from the Indian population by his participation in and identification with the national culture and his social consciousness.

Cholos are not accepted into the mainstay of mestizo society. With the heritage of a racist society, mestizos consider that the skin of cholos is often too dark; the process of exogamy—marrying out to lighter-skinned women—is still too recent to affect the "lightening process" highly valued in criollo and mestizo culture, for that matter. Nonetheless, the cholo does emulate the dominant societies' values and patterns with regard to clothing, household, and machine equipment. Common-law marriages among cholos are most frequent, although people do value church and civil marriages, which they generally cannot afford. A high value is placed on large families, a source of protection in old age, when, it is hoped, adult children will take care of their aged parents.

The only community activity I observed during 1968–1969 was the minga, a cooperative group that could work on such projects as repairing community bridges. The Roman Catholic church is very much present in the community, and baptizing a child (generally at age three, when he has survived childhood illnesses) entails finding someone in a higher social category to stand up as godparent in the parents' hopes of future special favors, loans, a feast, and so forth.

THE SPANISH CONQUEST

When compared to the rest of Peru, the Amazon was opened to Western influence rather late. Penetration of the jungle region by the Peruvian national state was not an easy task due to the inaccessibility of vast tracts of land that lay to the east of the high Andes Mountains. During the sixteenth century, however, some Spanish exploration did occur when tales of the existence of the fabulous land of El Dorado was said to lie toward the east. When the Spanish Conquest began in 1534, the fortune-seeking, adventure-bound captains of the Spanish explorers such as Pizarro were driven by two common ambitions: their desire to gain wealth and their desire to govern a territory of their own. Several expeditions set out from the coast to find El Dorado, to little avail. Around Iquitos, a permanent administrative political center was not established until 1861. Prior to this, intermittent Augustinian, Jesuit, and Franciscan missionaries attempted to subjugate dispersed Indian groups.

There were wars of Indian extermination in the mid-nineteenth century. With the rubber boom in the latter part of that century, this situation changed. A large European migration as well as a local exodus took place. People flocked to the jungle to get rich quickly by extracting the black gold—rubber—from the heart of the forest. The growth of the city of Iquitos was due to this boom, and the rural areas around it took on their present-day character of isolated hamlets, separated from one another by enormous distances due to the nature of the rubber-extracting techniques and working of the rubber trees.

When the Spanish arrived, they found root-crop agriculture, slash-and-burn technology, and bitter *manioc* as the mainstay of the food supply. In many areas, there were effective river craft, hammocks used as beds, the manufacture of pottery, and the use of elaborate fish poisons. Among both Indians and cholos, the use of the buoyant balsa tree rafts enabled river groups to travel over fearsome rapids in order to transport forest products from one region to another. Today, the rafts are resold as flooring for thatched houses in Belen. Historically, the women were the mainstay of agriculture, after men cleared virgin forests by burning trees to plant crops. Houses among the native peoples consisted of large, communal dwellings called *malocas,* which could contain as many as seventy residents. Geometric abstract art was widely diffused throughout the region. There was no formal government among the native peoples, but, rather, a headman functioned in an advisory capacity. Focus on private property was rather minimal, and even today it is not unusual, when visiting native enclaves, to see houses without walls, doors, or locks—just balsa flooring and thatched roofs (made from the palm tree).

Native peoples had a highly developed pharmacopoeia of medicines and herbs, which they used in healing, as well as numerous hallucinogens, including ayahuasca. Shamans were highly valued, and there existed elaborate beliefs concerning the spirit world. Most healing plants were believed to have a mother spirit with whom the healer could communicate. The shamans operated primarily as doctors and some acted as detested sorcerers. As part of their medical kit, there were emetics, purgatives, vapor baths, and remedies using ant bites, which enhanced a person's immune system. The paraphernalia of curing was quite complex.

THE CITY OF IQUITOS

To best understand the cholos who frequented the fortune-telling curiosos in Iquitos, a word on the city is in order. Iquitos is a virtual island in the jungle. It is an Amazonian port used by both large ocean vessels from Europe and commerce vessels: heavily laden canoes filled with jungle produce. Iquitos was a shiny, cemented city of 125,000 at the time of my study in 1968–1969. Today, its population is half a million. On a return visit in 2007, I found large areas of the slum's periphery filled with two-story concrete buildings. The market had quadrupled in size due to population pressure. Consumer goods arrived in large ocean liners and were offered for sale in small shops along the main street. Its sizable middle-class population consisted of shopkeepers, government employees, army personnel, small-scale artisans, and blue-collar workers. Today, industrial activity is minimal, but there are many contacts with the industrialized coast. There are also numerous daily air flights, both to the capital city, Lima, and

Figure 3.2. Scenes of Iquitos

to other Amazonian cities. Yet the character of the city is best seen in the twenty-one or more urban squatter settlements such as Belen, which encircle the city and house thousands of migrants who have left their jungle hamlets in search of work and opportunities for their children.

THE AMAZON TODAY

We are indebted to the research of the Peruvian writer and journalist Roger Rumrill, who in his recent book, *La Amazonia Peruana* (published under the auspices of the United Nations Development Program—UNDP), gives us an update on current issues in this part of the world. What emerges from Rumrill's studies and compilation of information presents the Beleño with an even less predictable world than forty years ago. Rural poverty has increased, with half of the Amazon population continuing to live in extremely destitute conditions. There is a poor use of natural resources. Historically, over the past five hundred years, indigenous communities were massacred and almost exterminated in the Amazon. Their population decreased from three hundred thousand to perhaps around fifty thousand. Western diseases brought by the Europeans caused a great loss of life. By the end of the nineteenth century, the Amazon experienced a rubber boom for the latex in its famous trees. Seeds were smuggled out of Peru to Britain and eventually to Southeast Asian plantations. In rural areas of Peru, 70 percent of the people suffer from malnutrition. Though the Amazon region represents some 59 percent of the total national territory, only 13 percent of the Peruvian population lives in this region.

The jungle is a major reserve of gas, sweet water, and a genetic bank of animal and plant species, and there has been petroleum exploration in the area. Nonetheless, much of indigenous knowledge has managed to survive. It is in amusement and fortune-telling that some of the shamanic beliefs in divination have been able to survive over the last several centuries. Today, with abrupt climate change, contamination of the rivers due to infusions of mercury in the gold extraction process, nutritional problems, and rural poverty, the condition of the cholo is worsening. Some 65 percent of that population has only a primary education. The natural ecosystems have eroded, and there is a loss of biodiversity. In the exploitation of oil by multinational companies, contamination of rivers and oceans has accelerated, and many biological species are becoming extinct. Deforestation on a massive scale has increased, and there is a real global ecological instability.

BELEN: THE STRUCTURE OF A SLUM

As we've seen, Belen is situated on the Amazon River at the foot of the city of Iquitos. The shantytown itself is set upon an eroding palisade some two hundred meters above sea level. Each year, jungle lands adjoining the community give way to urban growth due to population pressures. There is one major road that connects the shantytown to a small city, Nauta, about sixty miles from Iquitos, where many ayahuasca healers have centers. The Amazon River system serves as the major route of communication apart from somewhat costly daily air services from Iquitos to other Peruvian cities.

In this book, I use the concept of the ethnographic present tense. That is, I speak with a contemporary voice, although my work as an anthropological fortune-teller took place more than forty years ago. When I returned for visits in 1979, and then again in 2008, population pressures had caused tremendous increases and now Iquitos has nearly a quarter of a million residents, yet life appears to continue in the pattern I previously described in my research.[1] The slum of Belen continues to endure exceedingly high unemployment rates, excessive malnutrition, family breakdown, prostitution, vandalism, chronic illness, and other social pathologies. This sets the stage for a different kind of social analysis. When I lived in Belen, I found that I was familiar with people who did not know most of their neighbors, nor did they have any shared community traditions. Family unions were

Figure 3.3. A wake in Belen

fragile, and relationships between the sexes were explosive and filled with tension.

Because of extreme economic insecurity that occurs due to lack of jobs and the unavailability of jungle lands to farm, men and women work mainly at commercial activity tied to the movement of jungle produce to the city market located above the river's-edge slum. There is small-scale wholesaling of such produce, which necessitates a small amount of capital. Vegetables, fish, and other jungle products are resold again in the city market for insubstantial profit. The wholesalers are called *rematistas,* which is the largest occupational group in Belen. Others favored with accumulated capital own motor-powered boats that they load with staples such as rice, sugar, coffee, and gasoline. These entrepreneurs, called *regatones,* ply the many river inlets and sell their staples to river hamlet residents at a considerable markup. Numerous jungle farmers also devote time to hunting precious animal pelts that they sell to merchants in Iquitos, which then forward them to luxury stores in Europe or the United States. As the farmers carry pelts long distances to docked boats, they leave behind protein-rich meat to rot in the jungle. Other men work at tropical fish extraction, which brings in a small cash income. Because little time is left to farm their lands, these families become needy buyers of the food staples that the regatones bring on their monthly calls.

The barriada of Belen is flooded at least about four months per year. During this time, houses must either be abandoned or, if they are built on balsa-log supports or on an actual balsa raft, they rise with the water level. Householders must use canoes to get around or pay children to ferry them to market. Fishermen used to work near to home in the waters of the nearby Itaya River, but as populations have grown and as fishing has become indiscriminate, natural resources have been fast disappearing. The women and children stay alive as best they can by reselling produce in the market. Children work at odd jobs to help their mothers. Unlike other urban slums in Latin America, male outmigration is relatively small and pertains to less than 30 percent of the population. Other jungle areas, too, are economically depressed, and jobs are not easily available. Lima, the national capital, is far away and is costly to reach, and it is expensive to live there.

At the time when I did my fieldwork in Belen, sociologists had created a few surveys of slum residents.[2] Regarding affluence in Belen, only 8 percent of the population had motor boats, only 17 percent had canoes, only 14 percent had kerosene stoves, only 5 percent had refrigerators, only 17 percent had electricity, only 14 percent had access to clean drinking water—but 52 percent had sewing machines (pedal operated) and 47 percent had transistor radios. Half the population lived in common-law relationships.

MARGINALITY IN
THE CULTURE OF POVERTY

Because there is little major industrial activity in Iquitos, most Beleños live from jungle extractive activity in one form or another. Salaries and income, when available, derive from employment with government agencies, the army, and day labor involved with the exploitation of

Figure 3.4. Woman preparing masato, an alcoholic drink

Figure 3.5. Musicians

jungle resources. Beleños find it hard to break out of this cycle of poverty. These peasant farmers, now living in cities, are in a very marginal position. They try to cope with feelings of hopelessness and despair as they realize the improbability of achieving success in terms of the values and goals in the larger mestizo society. Most of these people are without land to farm or produce to sell.

LOVE MAGIC AND THE NAIPES

In this chapter, I look at elaborate systems of love magic predominant in this community and relate such beliefs to the harsh economic facts of life in order to understand better the impetus for Beleños to seek answers through the use of the naipes and those curiosos who helped them make sense of their fragile lives.

Throughout my year of study, as I read fortunes in Belen, I was overwhelmed by the sheer number of women who sought a reading of the fortune-telling cards in their desire to regain their husbands or boyfriends who had abandoned them, left them with children, or generally just toyed with their affections. Despite the fact that I was not proactive

Figure 3.6. Market in Chiclayo with naipes pamphlets for sale

in any way (and showed no interest in having a partner), as a single woman in my late twenties, my women friends in the community tried hard to find me a mate. One young woman took me to see two different curiosos who read my cards, using a deck similar to the one I used but reading all of the cards. (I personally felt that my style of reading was much less demanding than reading the entire deck of 40 cards.)

After the first four months of documenting in my notes recipes for how to find and keep a mate, I met my future husband, Yando, and subsequently moved into a balsa house in Belen with him. All the love magic recipes formerly given to me by my neighbors immediately came to an abrupt end. Dried up. In this section, I present some of the beliefs of Beleños in order to explain their dependence on the cards to provide them with peace of mind about the return of a loved one or the answer to many of their pressing questions regarding economic and emotional support. These beliefs are related to the insecurity, uncertainty, and despair in social interactions that are part of their everyday life. Magic is known for the attempt of individuals—both practitioners and believers—to control or manipulate the unknown. Using orations, spells, and charms allows many Beleños to put to rest all anxiety and insecurity, which then rewards the believer with hope and the assurance of success in a particular endeavor.

THE CULTURE OF POVERTY AND LOVE MAGIC IN BELEN

Though at first glance Belen might appear to be a tourist's paradise, with picturesque thatched floating houses, spectacular sunsets, and the like, it can in fact be linked to what has been called the culture of poverty by Oscar Lewis. Poverty in Belen contaminates all walks of life. We see how men toil at subsistence activities, working as laborers, unloading balsa rafts or boats full of jungle produce to be sold in the market. Others work as rematistas, and on a small scale they sell products brought to Belen—fish, plantains, fruits, and vegetables—in order to make a small profit. Accumulating capital is difficult, and daily activities to survive consume all the energies of the poor. Women have numerous children. There is only one faucet for potable water in the community of twelve thousand people, and it is situated more than a kilometer from the center of Belen.

Oscar Lewis wrote about Mexico and Puerto Rico, but he could easily have been focusing on Iquitos' slums. This culture of poverty transcends national boundaries and provides its members with a pattern of life, values, goals, and ideology. Feelings of despair, desperation, and fatalism and the breakdown of family structure characterize daily life in Belen. This way of life is an adaptation to the extremes of poverty and to an individual's marginal condition in a society that is highly individualist. This poverty influences the individual, particularly his dependence on magic and fortune-telling to aid in making decisions and alleviating anxiety.

When we look closely at the relationship between genders, we can see how the circumstances of poverty give rise to magical beliefs regarding love and acquiring and keeping a mate. A large number of women who pay to have their fortunes told are most concerned with abandonment by a lover or husband. Both men and women use a number of talismans and techniques to find a spouse or secure the love of a desired man or woman who may be uninterested in them. There is a tremendous amount of insecurity, uncertainty, and desperation in social relations, which are part of daily life. There are special diets that some women follow, such as eating only plantains and fish, which are said to ensure that a former lover returns to your side in fifteen to thirty days. Healers blow tobacco smoke over their client's head and shoulders. Recent research by my colleague Dr. Gehricke at the University of California, Irvine, has found that secondary smoke in some population samples can reduce anxiety and stress.

Men are said to mistreat their women, to get bored, and to leave one woman for another. Their reproductive strategy is to spread their seed as frequently as possible, yet far too often they may not provide economic support for their children. Because so much income in this part of the world is generated by extractive industries, men are accustomed to moving around to take advantage of supply and demand in relation to the availability of rainforest products. This entails long absences from their families. During the year I was in Iquitos, population pressures caused the yields of local fish to diminish. Fishermen therefore had to spend six weeks or more far away from the city in order to bring back their catch with the aid of dry ice. Women had to make do with market sales to sustain themselves and their families while husbands were away, which caused them great hardship.

We will explore four types of love magic in this part of the world: benign magic, malignant magic, preventive magic, and restitutive magic.

Benign magic includes hexes, orations, and techniques that do not menace anyone but are used in order to link a partner to the perpetrator at her side; such a partner may have abandoned the hearth or was planning to do so.

Malignant magic is carried out by an individual who does damage to another in order to reconquer a former lover or spouse who has absconded with another person. This type of love magic causes affliction, illness, or bad luck.

Preventive magic includes techniques that are prophylactic in order to prevent evil from occurring before the witch is successful. In this way, women often try to insure the possibility of obtaining a lover. The goal of this is to ascertain the availability of the man. Helped by a curiosa, a woman assures herself that malignant magic will not fall on her as the result of the bad intentions of the current lover or of the ex-wife of the man in whom she is interested.

The last category is *restitutive magic,* helped by healers or curiosos. (Some of these practice with ayahuasca, and others with invocations to the spirits they control.) Healers try to cure the illnesses and restore a natural, healthy balance in cases in which love magic has been responsible for a grave illness. We can see easily how reading the naipes is an essential element to prevent witchcraft from being leveled against a person or to eliminate illness believed caused by the malice of a lover, his former spouse, or some rival or angry person.

Much of this belief system falls within definitions of shamans all over the world, in societies where there exist beliefs that certain individuals have spirit familiars whom they can call upon to help their clients or harm their clients' enemies. Obviously, if the relationships between the genders were easy and took place in a climate of mutual confidence, there would not be such an elaborate typology of love magic. This is not the case in Belen. In this culture of poverty, notable for its high grade of social disorganization, broken homes, abandoned children, and prostitution, we see clearly that there are only two kinds of love: clean love and piggy love. Clean love includes sentiments of tenderness between men and women leading to sexual union. It never lasts. This is a fact of life according to informants. Piggy love (*amor cochinado*), which is a product of witchcraft, is the only form of love that persists. Such a simple polarization appears odd, but when we see the connection to the socioeconomic reality characterized by the alarming percentage of abandoned women and children who seek food handouts from the local Catholic church to ward off starvation or who die from tuberculosis due to malnutrition, these beliefs appear more logical.

ILLUSTRATIONS OF MAGICAL CATEGORIES

Love potions, called *pusangas,* which enable a person to obtain the love of someone, are known by the majority of members of the community. Men and women to whom I spoke in Belen often tell of magical techniques practiced by others. One young, abandoned mother who lived in a two-story balsa house depended for her maintenance on her fisherman father and her working mother. She showed me a small, regional bird called *tanrilla,* which she said she kept merely as a pet. This bird had long legs and claws. As a magical amulet, the bone of the foot was used as a type of telescope to look at the loved one. The client would look at the loved one through this telescope, taking care not to be seen. The next day she would have to avoid salt and lard. Due to the success of this spell, the love object would then fall madly in love with her. If, however, the object of this practice saw who was trying to seduce him, the magic would revert against the seducer, casting the spell with heightened potency. The protagonist would then become obsessively and antagonistically in love with the one who was the object of this magic!

Another example of benign magic is the use of a fragrant leaf called *congorillo*. Doña Jovita, a mother of nine children, confided in me that the secret of the success of her marriage that lasted many years (not at all common in Belen) was that she washed all her husband's clothing in a concoction made with this leaf. In this way, he couldn't abandon her. Even if he knew what she did, and even if he wanted to leave her, he would be incapable of doing so.

Benign magic frequently uses the genitals of the dolphin (*Delphinos restratus*), common in the surrounding rivers. It is said that the genitals of the female dolphin are physically very similar to those of human females. This skin flap is dried by a man who hides it in his arm or in the palm of his hand. Should he then "accidentally" touch the loved one in a greeting, such a woman would fall madly in love with him. As with the tanrilla, he must be careful that his feelings do not come to light. Moreover, he must abstain from certain foods and hide out for a day until the spell produces its desired effect. One woman that I spoke to told me that under the effects of ayahuasca, she saw this drama unfold. My woman friend who took me to have my cards read by other curiosos told me that the dolphins live under water in a beautiful setting upside down. They come out at night, change into well-dressed Christian men, with suits and ties, and go dancing in the hopes of luring young women to the river's edge, where they drag them down to live with them under the water.

Seeking in the category of malignant love magic are vengeful people who intend to cause suffering or disgrace to another in matters of love. Thus, a physical illness can be attributed to the bad faith of someone due to envy, for example, or due to rivalry, a slight, and so forth. Often, women believe they are bewitched by those who thought their loved one was being stolen away. Not infrequently, during a reading of the naipes, as one of her three questions, a client asks if the ex-spouse of her current lover has caused her whatever illness she may be experiencing. Generally, questions are not about how the client came to be ill, but rather, "Why me?" It is very clear that many cases of abandoned women fill the waiting rooms of curiosos as they search for the lovers who left them in order to make these men return home. For those who see a curiosa, the diagnosis is the first step before going to an ayahuasca healer, especially if it is clear that the husband is at fault or that his ex-wife is seeking revenge.

The third category, preventive magic, appears odd in that the client seeks magical help before something happens or before any damage occurs. In places such as Belen, full of insecurity and inundated with poverty, a woman has no option other than to vacillate before linking to a man. She must be sure he is not committed to another woman. Why look for more problems than already exist? If a man has another woman, linking to him will surely bring problems in the form of reprisals. Many curiosos and fortune-tellers are ready, for a small sum of money, to consult the naipes to find out if a would-be boyfriend has any attachments that might compromise him. In one case, a woman gave the curioso the name and address of her potential boyfriend, and the cards responded that he had another wife. At twenty-two years of age, this woman was already an abandoned mother with a child and decided not to pursue this romance.

The last category of love magic is restitutive. A large number of healers cure illness attributed to magical damage related to love. Again, many women go first to a curiosa to have the naipes read and to ask if their current illness is due to the evil of an ex-spouse of the beloved. It is much less expensive to have the answer to your question before shelling out large sums of money for a healer to reverse the evil.

The disintegration of this jungle community and the culture of poverty have given rise to a complicated and elaborate series of beliefs, values, and expectations that affect both men and women. The concept of love that lasts forever is not widely believed. The daily doses of misery can only exacerbate this dependence on magic.

In chapter 4, we will look at vignettes of clients I have seen that relate to this culture of poverty.

4

MARLENE, THE FORTUNE-TELLER

Seeing Magic from the Inside

When I first went to the coast of Peru in 1967 to study folk healing with the mescaline cactus, San Pedro, I saw pamphlets in the local markets near Salas in the city of Chiclayo. They advised interested parties on how to read the naipes cards. I was interested in learning how the cards played a role in the healing process. Because the healer, however, was not willing to share information with me, it was only by the good graces of a secretary of the university in Lima that I was shown how to read the naipes. At first I thought about the cards as entertainment. I had learned to read palms from a book on Hindu palmistry, and I was certainly open to fortune-telling. On occasion, I ate at a sandwich shop in downtown Manhattan that was right near the New York Public Library, and there, for the price of a cup of tea and a tuna sandwich, my tea leaves would be read.

While I was a graduate student at New York University, I attended classes at night and worked days selling tickets for a European airline company. One Christmas, I traveled to Paris and had my fortune told by a Gypsy woman with golden earrings. Everything she said miraculously came true, from the obvious "you will soon take an ocean journey" (my French accent wasn't that good), to a host of other predictions about romance.

Even though I was in anthropological training and identified myself as a social scientist, I was certainly open to learning about divination techniques. After my year in the Amazon, I realized that divination tools such as the naipes had a hidden structure.[1] Probability statistics that have to do with misfortune cards (see chapter 1) played an important role in diagnosing stressors and illnesses of the Beleños. Every day at sunset, I sat down in my balsa house and wrote up my notes and predictions. Because I lived in the community, I could informally see if some of the fortunes actually came true. In this way, I began to see how people remembered what suited them, and distorted, changed, or invented predictions that my notes showed I did not offer them.

One example was when a neighbor, Ariela, came to me to have her fortune told. She was a single mom with two little girls, one five years old and one an infant. She left her children alone so she could work at a market post above Belen in order to scrape out a meager existence. One day her baby girl became ill with fever. The day before, I had read her fortune, and the Ace of oro (diamonds) came up, indicating money. Then I left Belen for a few days to stay in my little apartment in the city in order to write up my notes. When I returned to Belen, I was told that I had predicted the death of the baby, which happened when I was away from the slum. Apparently, the baby's father came by to give Ariela some money for the baby's food that month, and this money was now being used instead for the wake and funeral. The good luck money card was transformed by the client into a prediction of death, which was unusual, because I never read that card to any of my clients. I knew that that they had enough problems without my adding to them.

Even though I had studied probability statistics in college and kind of enjoyed knowing about odds that could be applied to problem solving, I found myself hitting more and more on what my clients considered to be the truth of the reading. The language I used was always vague and nonspecific and thus open to interpretation. In the beginning, I practiced telling fortunes in Belen and never took any money for the readings. When I left for an anthropology meeting in Seattle, I was advised to do what other fortune-tellers did—namely, charge for the service. I kept my fee low, the cost of a kilo of rice, and far cheaper than my competition in the city of Iquitos itself. Little by little, when I rented a balsa hut moored to the Amazon on a main walkway, people wandered by, and many asked to have their fortunes told when they saw me doing a reading on the balsa open-air patio. No one took me seriously until I began to charge for the service.

A certain amount of skill was required to turn the separate items associated with each card into a story so that three or four cards read together presented a short narrative for the client. Furthermore, many of the cards had several diverse possible readings. In most cases, I had to choose the pertinent item that I thought applied to the man or woman before me. I found myself becoming more flamboyant, dramatizing my readings by hesitating at particular points and exclaiming at still others. Cautious with clients who possibly had evil in store and joyous when good news seemed forthcoming, I was quite drained emotionally after telling four or five fortunes in a row, as frequently was the case.

At first, I felt bad charging for the service. It seemed everything needed to survive in Belen had a price tag on it. I tried to rationalize collecting money in terms of the amounts I spent every week on medicine (I bought aspirin in thousand-lot bottles) and the gifts of food I always provided. I decided that every coin or two that I earned in a reading I would give to the nearest youngster to buy an ice cream or I would purchase medicines for distribution to Beleños as needed. Aside from the fact that my rates were cheap, the techniques adopted from others like me in the city were familiar to most of my clients. People were allowed to ask three questions of the cards, and they could ask anything they wished. The answer was either yes or no. My fame spread quickly. No longer did I have to stop people in the street to ask if they wanted me to tell their fortunes. Rather, hosts of people came to visit me, especially on Wednesdays, Saturdays, and Sundays—days considered propitious for fortune-telling. Women informants who considered themselves my friends operated as agents in the field without any prompting on my part. They would drum up business, and they often urged me to raise my prices, because, in their opinion, the readings were too cheap. Men would jump out of their canoes at dawn to ask that their fortunes be read before they made important business commitments.

Although some of my predictions came true, many more that I remembered and had logged in my notes did not. Repeat business frequently came my way, because I made it clear that the cards were temporal in nature, and that fortunes could always change. At the end of a day's hard labor, I found myself able to chat with neighbors about our shared fatigue, for I, too, was busy with insistent clients. My rented balsa house in Belen was well established now that I had a highly valued job in the community.

When I was in the midst of a reading, clients talked and commented on the identity of the various figures and events emerging in the reading—those good or evil people who could contribute to their luck. Tales of adultery, connivances, evil doings, hatred, opprobrium, and a host of emotions that might never be elicited from normal anthropological interviewing techniques flowed in a steady stream of conversations from my clients.

The most frightening aspect of my unconventional technique was the personal feeling, which I never quite shook, that despite my awareness of the fact that people forget information they don't like and often remember what is important for them, among my clients the cards never seemed to lie. I will examine two possible reasons for this in terms of intuition expertise studies in psychology as well as microcommunication from reading clients' facial expressions, of which apparently I had some skill. Hypnosis also plays a role worth exploring. (See chapter 4.)

During the time I was a fortune-teller, I never considered my actions as some kind of trick merely to get people to talk. Despite failures, many of the readings seemed to come true. Sometimes the cards frightened me when the death card or bad fortune turned up. The three questions at the end of readings often brought forth additional ethnographic material, which indicated just how close I had come to hitting the mark. One example was when I read the fortune of an elderly couple in their sixties. The card for land or nature came up, and somehow I interpreted it to read: "Your cattle will prosper." Mind you, this was a slum, with houses built almost one on top of another. The couple apparently had a small farm outside of Iquitos where they kept a few cows. The woman turned to be sure no one heard my prediction, and then said, "How did you know? No one knows! It's our secret." I don't know how I knew. Belen is full of secrets—envy is widespread and often causes people to keep their own counsel; malicious and envious individuals often seek witches to cause harm to others.

It was also interesting to note that when I read the fortune of young men and women, I invariably predicted data on love affairs and romantic interests. When older men and women were clients, illness, economic issues, and so forth often arose. One day, Maria, who was a grandmother—toothless and not particularly attractive—came to have her fortune read. She was full of family misfortune: her youngest daughter had run away from home with a soldier, and her oldest daughter was sick in bed with a postpartum infection. The cards predicted that a handsome man would come into her life. During the questioning period, she asked if his intentions would be honorable, and the answer was in the affirmative. When the reading was over, she turned to me and said, "Oh, Marlenita, you know that I'm too old for that sort of thing." I had to agree; her dignity was such that the term *amorous fury* in the medieval prose of the cards didn't seem to apply to her very well. I really thought the cards had made a mistake, but I said nothing more. Three weeks or so passed, and Maria returned. She listened patiently to the cards in this second reading but seemed anxious to ask the three questions. When that moment arrived, I was the one who was floored: she asked if her new boyfriend would move in with her. A self-fulfilling prophecy for sure!

As these types of incidents repeated themselves, I began to boast a bit about my successes, just as I had observed healers doing. After all, word of mouth in the slum, with a functional illiteracy rate of about 76 percent, was as effective as radio announcements on small transistor portables, which could be found everywhere. Successful predictions accumulated. By the end of my eighth month of fieldwork, the walk from the city market, which normally took me about ten to twelve minutes, began to take longer and longer as people began to tug at my sleeve and ask me to come into their houses to tell their fortune. One woman ran after me and, by way of introduction, said she had heard that I was the *gringa* who knew things.

People wanted their fortunes told in private. Celesta, originally from Brazil, had a very jealous husband. One day, early in my fortune-telling career, I settled in her run-down shack and began to tell her fortune when I noticed that my client was becoming visibly nervous and agitated. I didn't think it had to do with the fee. Generally, I took that coin at the beginning of the reading. If the client didn't like his fortune, I offered to return the money and thus negate the reading. I had to do that only on a few occasions. Celesta's house was full of neighbors, all women, because a heavy downpour had begun and no one wanted to venture out in the rain. Her agitation increased, especially as four Kings appeared, each of whom indicated a particular man with physical or emotional characteristics: generous, valiant, and so forth. She abruptly asked me to stop, which I did, thinking I had somehow offended her. Finally, the rain let up a bit and the other women left. My friend sighed with relief and told me of the problems she was having with these neighbors. Every time her husband returned from a fishing trip that lasted several weeks, these women went to him in secret and told him of the other boyfriends that Celesta supposedly had while he was away. She was certain that the evidence of the four Kings would be used by these vicious neighbors to further incriminate her.

In preparation for an article on the naipes, I had interviewed thirty women who paid me to read their cards. Listed here are the types of questions I was asked at the end of the readings. They illustrate the themes that troubled those women who sought my help.

Will my husband return to me? (3 queries)

Will I finish my schooling? (1 query)

Will I get married? (6 queries)

Are my boyfriend's intentions honorable? (1 query)

Does my husband have another woman? (4 queries)

Did my brother-in-law steal my money? (1 query)

Will my boyfriend return to me? (5 queries)

Will I continue to live with my boyfriend? (4 queries)

Will I have a baby? (4 queries)

Do my in-laws like me? (1 query)

Will my husband leave me? (3 queries)

What gender will my child be? (1 query)

Will I find work? (1 query)

Will I travel? (4 queries)

Will my child's illness get better? (1 query)

Will the guilty person pay for the motorcycle accident? (1 query)

Will my daughter marry? (1 query)

Will my sick relative get better? (3 queries)

Will my cattle increase in number? (1 query)

Will my ex-husband support the children? (2 queries)

Will my private thoughts come true? (3 queries)

Does a certain man I know have good intentions? (3 queries)

Will I continue to live with my mother? (1 query)

Will I have a good life? (1 query)

Men also asked a few usual questions of the cards.

Will I reunite with my girlfriend? (1 query)

Does my wife love me? (1 query)

Will I find work? (1 query)

Will I travel? (4 queries)

Will my girlfriend travel with me? (1 query)

Will my business partner return? (1 query)

INTUITION EXPERTISE AND
FORTUNE-TELLING IN THE AMAZON

While many people I know, including myself, like to think of themselves as intuitive, creative, and so forth, it is heartwarming to see that professional psychological research is paying more attention than ever to the concept of intuition.[2] The term *naturalistic decision making* (NDM) is used by academic psychologists to look at expert intuition, which sometimes is remarkably accurate and other times way off base. Arthur Simon defines intuition as the recognition of patterns stored in memory. He and others try to demystify intuition by looking at the cues that experts call upon to make their judgments. This occurs even if the cues involve tacit knowledge and are difficult for the expert to articulate. In terms of my own work as a curiosa, I spent countless hours learning to read the cards. Before coming to Belen, I had studied with engineering colleagues in Los Angeles to learn how probability statistics worked. I studied the fascinating history of the cards. Moreover, I lived in the slum of Belen and pored over the sociological surveys that documented life in the slum. I spent endless days going from houseboat to houseboat to interview residents and listen to their life histories. By the time I began to tell fortunes, I was immersed in the culture and very involved with the naipes.

Now the psychologists who study intuition recognize that the intuitive judgments of some professionals show impressive skill, while the judgments of other professionals show remarkable flaws. One woman I spoke to in Belen was very perplexed when an ayahuasca healer (obviously with flawed intuition) told her that an illness she suffered was due to the bewitchment of an ex-boyfriend from the *chacra,* or farm, where she lived before she came to Belen. She sat with me and was confused, for she was eighteen years old and didn't have an ex-boyfriend. The ayahuasca healer had really messed up, and she kept wracking her brain to find someone to fit the flawed interpretation of that one healer.

Unlike in evidence-based psychology, the criteria to judge expertise are based on a history of successful outcomes rather than on any measurement tests. In my case, the apparent vagueness of the readings, which people were able to apply to their own circumstances of life, set the stage for my reputation to grow. New clients kept coming, and my successes spread. I was seen as an expert who had the necessary skills and abilities to perform. In fact, skilled intuition is full of cues that give the expert access to information that is stored in memory, which provides answers for the client who is sitting in the reading. Intuition becomes a process of recognition. I also found myself using the subjunctive tense in my readings in Spanish. That tense always sounds poetic to me, and it also codes uncertainty. The equivalent in English would be *perhaps, maybe, might it be that* . . . giving me an escape hatch if something didn't come true. Moreover, people didn't take notes. (There was not much paper and few pencils in the slum.) Basically, the Beleños who sought their fortunes with me were selective in their memory. Thus, intuition is not acquired by any kind of rational process. Rather, it is skilled pattern recognition. Working as a psychotherapist today with managed care patients, I think some of the same skilled pattern recognition is at work in my practice. Sometimes women will come to see me when they are all choked up and find it difficult to talk. The few questions I ask about spouse and family are enough to start the words flowing, with repetitive themes of infidelity, alcoholism, neglect, and violence often coming to the fore.

Because I have always thought of myself as an intuitive person, I tried to understand why the label of *intuitive* characterized me and not someone else, for example. For a period in the 1980s, I was very interested in the literature on split-brain research—that is, the split between the two hemispheres of the brain and the psychological characteristics of both. Because I was a left-handed woman, some interesting aspects came to light. My visual-spatial processing was below average—perhaps in the 36th percentile—based on a psychological test I had taken in college. This was not much of a handicap, really, manifesting itself in my inability to pack the trunk of my car neatly before I left for vacation and in my not knowing how fax cartridges fit into the fax machine. As if to compensate for that, however, the relational aspects of my right brain (affected by my left-handedness) meant that I could readily see connections between one idea and another. After all, in split-brain research we know that one hemisphere controls the opposite part of the body—in my case, the right hemisphere controlled the left part of my body. Yet instead of housing visual-spatial schemata and objects in space, my right brain was filled with words in both hemispheres—words that enhanced pattern recognition!

Psychologists argue that creative intuition is based on finding valid patterns in memory, and some people are better than others at this task. I was pleased to learn that often even skilled judges are unaware of the cues that guide them. I always assume people know all that I know or have studied, and while in Belen, it was very difficult for me to articulate the successes I had in readings I made. Ahead, we'll look at still other explanations for the success of the naipes readings.

MICROMANAGEMENT OF FACIAL EXPRESSIONS

What happens when an anthropologist is perceived to be a person of metaphysical talent and knowledge within the culture she is studying? How do both the informants and the anthropologist react to this phenomenon? The social scientist who takes the trouble to learn the cultural symbols of divinatory systems such as the naipes becomes a performance agent in that culture. Of course, we have to be careful about the loss of objectivity, what the psychologists call *bias*. The journey is worth it, I think, for I had the opportunity to gain access to the personal feelings, expectations, and values of the Beleños.

The work of Paul Ekman[3] on micro-expressions of the face and body is important to help us see how traditional healers and curiosos learn about their clients' histories while appearing to be omnipotent. Emotional expression is an outward manifestation of inner states, and

Darwin early on in the nineteenth century provided the basic message that emotional expression functions in this way. Darwin spoke about emotions of relatively short duration, which are intentional states that cause changes in motor behavior and physiological and cognitive change in an individual. A sensitive individual can note postural changes and facial expressions, especially if he is trained in hypnosis, in which there is a constant need to monitor motor and cognitive feedback of the patient to the messages presented in the trance state. In fact, the hypnotherapist himself may actually go into trance during the client's induction.

As far back as 1972, Paul Ekman and his colleagues vindicated Darwin's ideas that emotional expressions are universal and directly associated with underlying emotional states. In fact, emotional facial expressions are viewed as communicative signals.[4] Ekman is one of several researchers on the cross-cultural consistency of emotional expression.[5] Ekman's work clarified for me the "successes" I had as a fortune-teller during my year of research. Emotions are about pleasure and pain, approach and avoidance. They are characterized by intensity and valence. Randolph Nesse and John Ellsworth wrote about unpleasant emotions such as tenseness, nervousness, stress, upset, sadness, and depression. These contrast to pleasant emotions such as alertness, excitation, elatedness, happiness, serenity, and relaxation. During my readings of the naipes, the emotional expressions of the Beleños were very open and near the surface. As the card readings brought forth the stressors and negative events in their lives, clients spoke along with the cards—exclaiming, showing happiness or sadness, suspicion or anger as evil was attributed to a particular significant other in the milieu who was faulted for bad luck, witchcraft, or simply downright malice. The title of my first article on the naipes drew on the term *fortune's malice* to indicate the overall gross negativity of the cards' messages. This contrasts with the control of our destiny that we will see revealed in part 2, in the exploration of Septrionism.

Ekman suggests that hardwired programs in humans link basic emotions such as happiness, sadness, fear, disgust, anger, surprise, and contempt. Such emotions are socially learned and recognized cross-culturally. In fact, Ekman coined the term *micro-expressions*. He postulated that appraisals of specific emotions are associated with specific facial movements, however brief, which invite scrutiny. He argued that these facial movements could last from one fifth to one twenty-fifth of a second and give us access to a person's true feelings. In my psychotherapy sessions each week in southern California, it is not unusual that, in the midst of a counseling session and seemingly out of nowhere, a client bursts into tears or becomes agitated. By listening carefully and being attentive to the micro-expressions of the face, a skilled therapist learns almost to predict when such a moment will arrive, and when the eyes will tear.

In the fortune-telling activity that I conducted during my fieldwork in Belen, I was seen to be a cultural specialist, a stranger who had come from far away, a stranger who was tall and who looked different. I wore gold hoop earrings and golf shoes to better negotiate the mud. While individuals are relatively stronger at recognizing emotional expressions from members of their own cultural group, the curiosa transcends that construct. I often felt that I was entering into a light hypnotic trance—perhaps a 2 on a scale of 1 to 6—along with my clients as I remained motionless and looked constantly in their direction. Because people were paying for their fortunes to be told, they had the right to be expressive.

SUGGESTIBILITY AND THE NAIPES

More and more evidence indicates that suggestibility is a psychological characteristic of altered states of consciousness. Anthropologists, unlike psychologists or psychiatrists, rarely use the term *suggestibility*. This is a concept that indicates a person's propensity to respond to suggested communications or that indicates a particular state of mind that is favorable to suggestion. H. J. Eysenck defined *suggestion* as a process whereby one or more people cause one or more individuals to change without the critical response of their judgments, opinions, attitudes, or patterns of behavior.[6] Psychologists show interest in who elicits suggestibility. Is the communicator a high-status individual? Moderate levels of anxiety increase social influence. Suggestibility is an adaptive mechanism that allows the individual the capacity for denial, illusion, and false or overly optimistic beliefs, which enable the person to cope with stress and conflicts. We human beings may be suggestible due to our survival needs.[7] When we enter into these states we can transcend reality, create social cohesion, and allow emotional discharge. What Simon has called *bounded rationality* is a human tendency to learn from others or to accept social influence through docility, which contributes to our ability to survive.

The so-called magical results of fortune-telling appear to have underlying rational explanations. Whether through the interpretation of misfortune cards, which are highly likely to appear in any given reading, or the reader's examination of emotions through perceptions of micro-expression and muscular movement in clients' facial expressions or a form of hypnotic trance and suggestibility, we can look closely at how magic works. Perhaps science is catching up with magic.

In part 2, we will turn to another Peruvian manifestation of destiny—this time, linked to teachings of the Sacred Mystical Order of Septrionism in Peru and abroad.

PART TWO

Destiny and Personal Control

Septrionic Concepts in Mysticism

5

THE SACRED MYSTICAL ORDER OF SEPTRIONISM

A Peruvian Spiritualist Religion

In this chapter, we will look at the history of mysticism in Peru and its influences from Europe and the United States. The history of spiritualism is important to understand in order to set Septrionism within a worldwide context. Then we'll turn to the doctrines of the Septrionism organization and writings of Shikry Gama (the spiritual name of Claudio Cedeño) on destiny and poverty—which contrast dramatically with the beliefs of the Beleños regarding lack of control over their own lives and being.

MYSTICISM

First, we should define the term *mysticism* itself. Generally, it refers to the experience of unity or apprehension of an ultimate nonsensuous unity in all things, a oneness or One, which neither sense nor reason is able to penetrate.[1] Historically, the mystic's life was seen as a recognition of the existence of the inner personal experience, which was independent of and even antagonistic to social reality.[2]

French psychiatrist Jean-Pierre Valla pointed out that until recent years, mysticism was believed to be an uncommon phenomenon restricted to especially endowed or favored individuals—for instance, religious figures such as St. Teresa of Avila.[3] Some sociological studies in the United States and England, however, have shown that 20 to 40 percent of randomly selected adults claim at some time in their lives to have intense experiences, which they consider religious.[4] Certainly, New Age religions such as those written about by Paul Heelas show that there is a proliferation of special techniques to achieve naturally induced altered states of consciousness.[5] Psychologists and psychiatrists have recently replaced theologians in discussing the validity of such states as part of normal functioning versus pathological states.[6] There have been controversies over the validity of the mystical experience, which has always been held as suspect by religious bureaucrats.

Psychiatry is not quite clear on what to do about mysticism. In preparation for publishing the 1980 version of the Diagnostic and Statistical Manual III, the Group for the Advancement of Psychiatry published a report that viewed mystical experiences and those who sought them out as pathological. Others, such as the psychiatrist Arthur Deikman, criticized this partisan position.[7] It is easy to view mysticism as deviant because there are few organized mystics to lobby in favor of their beliefs.

HISTORY OF SPIRITUALISM IN LATIN AMERICA

There has been an enormous gap between tribal shamanism and the influence of Christianity in the Amazon over the last four hundred years. More recently, there has been a development of spiritualist philosophies, which originated in the United States and Europe in the nineteenth century.

Christian influence is notable in this part of the world. Historically, Christian missionaries have been in Peru since the 1600s and actively proselytized native peoples. The Bible is full of elements regarding trance states, and in 1 Corinthians, Jesus speaks of how the righteous can discern spirits—congruent with Septrionic beliefs.

Spiritual doctrines found their way to cities such as Iquitos and Pucallpa during the rubber boom of the late nineteenth century and were influenced by the growing discontent in nineteenth-century Europe. It may be tempting to think about the Amazon as an earthly enclave far away from the maddening roar of intellectual ideas or philosophical tendencies in religion, medicine, or science, but this is not the case. Darwin's doctrines of evolution spread throughout the world after 1859, and science was viewed as a way to provide all answers to humanity's predicaments. Religious beliefs declined while respect for science surged. In the second half of the twentieth century, there was a reaction against and disillusionment with science. Materialism made its impact, and a spontaneous search arose for a transcending quality to triumph over rationality and the cold impersonal objectivity of mechanistic science.

Though *spiritism* and *spiritualism* appear linked, there are real differences between them. The doctrine of spiritism in general argues that all that exists is spirit and that departed spirits are able to communicate with mortals. By entering into nonusual mental states such as trance, a medium is able to communicate with spiritual entities on behalf of his clients.[8] There is some similarity between spiritism and shamanism, because the shaman's omnipotent powers discern such spirit forces and subsequently dominate and control them for the shaman's own needs and purposes, particularly for his clients. The shaman, however, is generally thought of as a moral arbiter of society who works on behalf of his client and harms that person's enemies, if necessary.

In Europe and the United States, the nineteenth century was a time in which spiritualism reached its heyday, with spirit communications, materializations, and table knockings widely reported in the press and popular books in the 1840s.[9] Before this period, Anton Mesmer and his theories of animal magnetism polarized European intellectual thought, especially because Mesmer was one of the first to treat disease without claiming access to religious authority. By 1850, spiritualism had spread throughout the United States, England, Europe, and Latin America. The first glimmerings of its impact in Latin America came from Guatemala and Cuba in the 1850s. By 1865, spiritualism was found in Caracas, Venezuela, among high government officials who claimed to have contact with spirits of the highest order.

The major intellectual influence on Latin American spiritualism was Allan Kardec (1804–1869), the nom de plume of Leon Rivail, who published many books and articles on the subject, which were translated into Spanish and widely distributed throughout Central and South America. Kardec disdained the term *spiritualism,* because it had been so widely used. For him, the term meant simply anyone who believed that a realm exists that contains more than matter, but did not necessarily indicate a belief in spirits. Kardec's main focus was to demonstrate the existence and immortality of the soul. He used the term *spiritism* rather than *spiritualism* to argue that the spiritualists dealt only with occult phenomena, while the beliefs of spiritism were that of a religion. According to Kardec, spiritism is a philosophy and a science that is compatible with all religions. Differences in doctrines exist between the two groups, but the terms often crop up indistinguishably. The anthropologist Sidney Greenfield, who has worked with Brazilian spiritists,[10] writes about the belief of Kardec that when the Judeo-Christian-Islamic creator God made the universe, he established two dimensions of reality. One was material, which the sciences have developed to enable us to comprehend. The other dimension was of the spirit. In Kardec-influenced doctrines, spirits move between the two domains and animate both. Though they live on the spirit plane, they periodically assume material bodies to come to this world. After a period of time, they disincarnate and leave their bodies, returning to the spirit world, where they live lives similar to ours.

Hindu influences were very strong in Kardec's writings, and he believed in the concept of reincarnation and karma. The latter states that nothing in life is fortuitous and that we cannot escape the consequences of our actions.

Early spiritualists in the United States were influenced by Emanuel Swedenborg, a Swedish mystic who lived from 1688 to 1772. An engineer and metallurgist by profession and a highly educated man, he wrote thirty-two books on the world of the spirit. His message was that our life depends on our relationship with a hierarchy of spirits. All of life corresponds to a hierarchy of beings, which represent different orders and yet act in correspondence with one another. Swedenborg, like other mystics, recognized that breathing exercises and introspective concentration were essential to realize mystical unity experiences. The practices he developed resemble the yogic *pranayama* (breath control) and *pratyahara* (withdrawal). Both are calculated to awake inner awareness and to break awareness barriers between the world of human beings and the spirits.

Swedenborg influenced spiritism and spiritualism in his writings because he wrote about both high and low spirits. The low spirits seek to possess and control some part of a person's body. The higher-order spirits are more rare and do not oppose the person's will but instead are helpful guides. Swedenborg conceptualized them as angels who assist us. Many of the spirits reside in the interior mind, and good spirits have some control over evil ones. Both the spiritualists and spiritists philosophically can be named idealists. They emphasize the primacy of the spiritual over the material. Throughout Latin America, Kardec's doctrines filtered down to the urban lower classes and peasantry and mixed with Afro-Cuban cultures and folk Catholicism in the Caribbean and Brazil.

Kardec's doctrines included communication with the world of spirits via mediums and the idea—similar to Christian dogma—that the soul survives after death. Reincarnation exists, and there is no belief in the devil or hell. Human beings are said to comprise three parts: a material body, which perishes with death; a fluid body or a spirit wrapping or embryo that separates from the body during sleep, hypnosis, and trance; and a perfectible and imperishable spirit.

Spiritism diffused widely throughout Latin America. It originated in the United States with the famous Fox sisters and table rappings in upstate New York in the 1840s* and spread to all parts of Europe. Because many Latin American middle-class youth were educated in Europe and in Paris by preference, Kardec's direct influence was felt on Latin American esoteric thought. Kardec's philosophy gained a large number of followers in Mexico, Brazil, Argentina, and other countries. In Peru, the doctrine's main route of diffusion was in the Amazon region, owing to that area's predominant cultural exchanges with Europe, rather than with the Peruvian capital of Lima. Lack of roads and easy access by ships from the Atlantic Ocean via the Amazon River to Iquitos and Brazilian cities such as Manaus furthered this diffusion. Many spiritist centers were established in Iquitos and elsewhere.

SEPARATION OF SPIRITISM
AND SPIRITUALISM

In spiritism, experience is rooted in the belief that it is possible to communicate with spirits by means of diverse medium-related phenomena. Kardec argued for the possibility that any afflicted person can communicate with a beloved being who has died. The spirit of that deceased person might take the body of the medium by means of incorporation during a brief period of time in order to converse with his living relatives. Christianity, in its early years, rejected the belief in communication with the world of spirits. Prior to around the fourth century CE, there was a popular belief that all adherents could communicate with Jesus or his apostles. A group of people arose—historically known as Charismatics—who said they had communicated with the spirit of the Lord and had received revelations.[11] They believed that this communication with the spirit of Jesus was a gift that God conceded to the

---

*[The Fox sisters, Margaret, Kate, and Leah, played an important role in the creation of spiritualism by claiming that they communicated with spirits. In 1888 Margaret confessed that the "rappings" were a hoax but later retracted her statement. —*Ed.*]

faithful. Yet the propagation of this practice created chaos in the faith of these believers. There were many contradictions in the revelations, which seemed to serve human passion rather than divine design. These personal communication reports greatly split the authority of the early church hierarchy. Officials had no alternative but to prohibit this communication with spirits, calling it satanic because of the disorder and confusion of faith that it occasioned. These prohibitions increased with the centuries and culminated in the horrors of the Inquisition, which combated everything that fell under the name of occultism and witchcraft, called diabolic practices, and often resulted in burning at the stake. The church slowly realized that it was necessary to assemble many proofs of authenticity and veracity among those canonized in order to accept the divine communications and miracles of those chosen people.

Yet there also developed the practice of following a virtuous life inspired by the teachings of "love thy neighbor," charity, and the forgiveness of sins. The totality of these practices has, until now, been known as spiritualism, which did not correspond to the mediumistic experience of the Catholic followers of Allan Kardec.

Brother Claudio (Shikry Gama), in his adolescence, frequented spiritist circles and recognized that mediums had existed since the origin of humankind. There are and will always be people who are gifted with paranormal faculties, which permit them to mediate between incarnated and disincarnated spirits. Kardec favored the practice of the incorporation of spirits into a medium in order to facilitate communication with his adepts. Septrionism proscribes this incorporation, which does not guarantee authentic communication.

Brother Claudio defines the mystic (he doesn't talk about mysticism) as an attitude of human beings that, through service, meditation, and perceptions from a person's cognitive intelligence, clarifies the understanding of the laws of nature and perceives the presence of the Divine in the things of the surrounding world, sublimating the person's spirit until he obtains union with his causal essence.

There is a real difference between the mediumistic experience per se and the experience of a life dedicated to the practice of the norms and postulates of a religious doctrine and the individual's consequent dedication to the study of the life beyond. In the writings of Brother Claudio, spiritualism as used in Septrionism implies the cultivation of our daily life of moral virtues and ethics. It is a way of life not conditioned to the necessity of paranormal communication with divinity. It certainly doesn't exclude all the sensory or extrasensory possibilities that the mind can perceive, as we saw with reading the naipes, but neither does it sustain this as a condition of it. In fact, extrasensory activities can be a hindrance to spiritual evolution if they are used as a means in itself. The essence of spiritualistic doctrines of exemplary lives is found by rendering service to our fellow humans, in salvation of the soul, perfection of the spirit, and the evolution of values.

Needless to say, every religious doctrine acknowledges the possibility of realizing an exemplary life and reaching a high spiritual plane among the characteristics of its beliefs. This doesn't suppose that every believer, by the mere fact that he agrees to follow that doctrine, is able to acquire a spirituality in his life that the moral norms exact. Recognition of such spirituality is based on examples rather than arguments.

Looking at spiritualism as a philosophy, we see that we must practice an exemplary life. Spiritism, on the other hand, demands only participation in the practice of mediumship or other rites without necessarily establishing beforehand the perfection of our life. The majority of the followers of spiritism tend to postpone the development of virtues and the potentialities of the individual intelligence. They often submit to a dependent fanaticism regarding spirit communications and negate their natural intellectual capacity to discern, to arrive at a decision, and to make a choice in order to resolve the common problems of human survival. This includes the concept of destiny, which we will examine from a Septrionic approach in chapter 6. Under special circumstances, spiritists may have experienced paranormal events, which confirm to them that the spirits of beyond have come to help the living and have manifested themselves miraculously. Allan Kardec's teachings postulated the growth of certain virtues in the lives of his adherents, which was especially necessary for those who were to become mediums or "operators." Spiritist groups no doubt exist. These groups reunite moral values and spirituality, and members of these groups do communicate with special spirits.

There are many writers who use the two terms—*spiritualism* and *spiritism*—indistinguishably to refer to the phenomenon of communication with the world of spirits. The discussion of the differences between the two terms in Shikry Gama's writings is seen as necessary to eliminate confusion in the distortions that occur in the interchange of the terms without any distinctions. A spiritualist, according to Septrionism, can experience diverse grades and forms of paranormal communication with the beyond without the necessity of mediumistic incorporation of a spirit into a borrowed body. All that's required, by contrast, to be a spiritist is to practice mediumship, whether as a follower of a group, as a medium, or as an operator. It is not necessary to possess special virtues. Mediumship can occur by means of total or partial incorporation of the spirit, or it can take on other forms such as automatic writing or auditory or telepathic channels.

Important to note, however, is that the faculty of being able to communicate with the spirits of the beyond does not convert a person into a spiritualist. Any needy person, whether of good or doubtful morality, can practice and believe in spiritism without this belief guaranteeing that his life will acquire exemplary habits. Moreover, spiritism can evoke the presence of good or tenebrous spirits (mostly lower-level spirits) and can do as much evil as good. Spiritualism, on the other hand, by its nature and virtues, permits only the practice of good toward our fellows. Spiritists can also experience other forms of communication, and by being virtuous can conceivably convert themselves into spiritualists. We must not confuse the phenomenal reality of spirit communication through mediumship with another reality that stresses the virtues of exemplary behavior in human relationships.

SEPTRIONISM IN PERU

Septrionism was born in the Amazon during the spring of 1968 as the result of revelations that emanated from the spiritual world—what the Peruvian mystic and philosopher Shikry Gama calls the *astral plane.*

Claudio Cedeño Araujo (Shikry Gama)

Founder of the Sacred Mystical Order of Septrionism

Claudio Javier Cedeño Araujo was born June 8, 1936, in Iquitos, Peru, to a family of Spanish descent. His father was Colombian and his mother Peruvian. At two and a half years of age, at the insistence of his grandmother, he went to live with her to be raised and educated. He initiated his primary education at the San Agustin School in Iquitos and completed his high school at the Benavidez Unified School of Iquitos.

Since he was a child, Brother Claudio communicated with the spiritual world. With the instruction of guides, his uncle José Pelayo Araujo initiated him at five years of age into a spiritist circle called Medio Dia (Noon). Since Brother Claudio's youth, the spiritual guides insisted that he must fulfill the duty for which he was born. He was not to read books, in order to avoid religious and political indoctrination, thus not contaminating himself with confusion that would impede his perceptions and clarity of the reality of the physical and spiritual world.

After a period of rebelliousness, during which time he vainly attempted to avoid this responsibility, and after various frustrations due to unfulfilled socioeconomic opportunities, he finally experienced a nine-month retreat at the edge of the Amazon River, during which he debated and engaged in dialogue with the spiritual guides regarding the mission that awaited him to fulfill.

From the end of 1959 until 1962, Brother Claudio completed a pilgrimage that was a major life experience to serve those who required his help. During this period, he was not supposed to, nor was he able to, touch money or have more than one change of clothing. In this way, spreading his ideas to those who were interested, he arrived in Bogotá,

Colombia. There he met the first woman, Hermana Pepita Placey Gonzalez de Cedeño, who would accompany him as a missionary until her death in 1989. Brother Claudio married Nathalie Lopez Zondervan de Cedeño on February 14, 1992. She is personal secretary to Brother Claudio and officiants (Eonté) at Septrionic ceremonies in Lima. As the official commentator on Septrionic doctrine, she is dedicated to organizing the secretariat and administration of Septrionism and its doctrine.

In 1968, the Sacred Mystical Order of Septrionism was founded in Iquitos, and it officially initiated the spread of the teachings that the spiritual guides entrusted to Brother Claudio.

Originally entitled Brahamanism-Lamaism of the Amazon, the name was later changed to Septrionismo de la Amazonia. From the revelations Shikry Gama garnered from the astral plane, a new worldview was derived of the nature of the Divine and its universal laws, which embrace a wide mystical, social, and scientific spectrum, along with the practical means to achieve spiritual realization. Brother Claudio and his followers are mostly middle-class urban men and women. The purpose of the organization is to achieve coherence and unity among mystical, religious, and ethical and moral values and science. The doctrines of the group, like many philosophically oriented beliefs, are viewed as harmonic with modern science and not in opposition to science's methodology and theories about the nature of reality.

The founder saw Septrionism as a universal creed that elevates personal knowledge of the spiritual world as a primary aspect of the system. It is a contemporary mystical approach to self-knowledge and development. It sees its role as providing a new view of the world, delineating universal laws of causality and speaking to the questions of the mission of human beings in society and their relationship to eternal forces. Shikry Gama's doctrine is concerned with helping humankind to achieve change and spiritual peace and to overcome afflictions.

The people who gathered around these new ideas at a certain moment felt the necessity to organize themselves to create a propitious place in their drive to improve values. The organization comprises two mystical bodies: followers and those who serve.

The first group has only an obligation to find in Septrionic teachings the betterment of their moral and ethical values in order to realize their spiritual aspirations. Members of the second group devote themselves to the spiritual service of the mystical order. To enter Septrionism, we must study the doctrine. This includes understanding and incorporating a series of basic values into daily life. Followers respond to the needs of those who are interested in the doctrine yet who don't desire a commitment to affiliate with the organization. Septrionism doesn't believe that it is necessary for minors to become part of the Septrionic order because it is thought that in becoming so, their free will would be forced or coerced.

Another reason why children are not considered members is that the doctrine does not admit that human beings have been condemned by God to original sin. Due to causality and free will, Septrionism recognizes that human beings by their actions reward and punish themselves. It is human beings who condemn themselves to suffering. By their own actions, human beings turn away from the Divine. Yet human beings who act with rectitude are able to rescue themselves from this condemnation of suffering, adversities, and tribulations that produce errors. For this reason, all that human beings must overcome is ignorance.

Septrionism acknowledges that common sense and prudence of human reasoning is determined at the age of twenty-one. With respect to civic traditions, human rights, and the constitution of society, however, Septrionics accept the laws that emancipate members of society at eighteen years of age, recognizing these young people's capacity to exercise their rights of self-determination. This is a right that includes the just and legitimate attribute of choosing the faith or belief elected by a person of age according to civic tradition.

Spirituality in Septrionism

Septrionic spirituality is based on mysticism and the search for knowledge of reality by means of personal experience. It also includes becoming aware of our personal characteristics by means of sincere dialogue, the interchange of ideas, and our vital experiences. The purpose is to clarify our existential confusion, situating us always within natural laws and common sense achieved by humanity throughout time. Septrionics thus try to find their own path, to take responsibility for their own life and for their own actions. They avoid becoming dependent on others, because that damages us as individuals and invalidates us spiritually, thus depriving us of liberty. No one must impose upon us what we must do. Our duty is to learn to use our intelligence in order to identify, recognize, and discern that which we experience, feel, and think in order to know what we are, how we are, and who we are. Only in this way can we achieve fully the ability to develop ourselves.

As with all natural laws, human behavior is also subject to the laws of causality. Spirituality is achieved only to the degree to which we are able to dominate the causal effects of our behavior. For these reasons, in Septrionic mysticism, there is a search for the *egocausublimacion* (egocausublimation) of our spirit through the dominion and the control of the causality of our behavior. In this way, we learn consciously to manage our free will.

Most important is that we elect a path and practice it with rectitude. If we do, we will inevitably arrive at the essence of the Divine, tuning in to the energetic principles that govern the laws of nature.

Mysticism and Science

Septrionism reconciles mysticism and science, faith and reason. It demonstrates by means of its rational and scientific fundamentals that reason is not opposed to faith. Rather, reasoning must be a balance that examines the advantages and inconveniences of faith. Septrionism believes that science, rather than destroying the concept of the Divine, is in charge of proving the living presence of the Divine in all the manifestations of nature. This is so because the Divine is science and science is the only form to discover and to demonstrate its constitutive nature.

Lo Dios *(the Divine)*

Septrionism poses a total reform of the conception of the nature of God. The Divine is not a being but a conjunct of intelligent energies that by principles and evolutionary laws creates and maintains all the existence of all the universes. This God is called the Eon of Eternal Intelligence. Its constitution is of a matter of a dimension that vibrates faster than the speed of light. The nature of Eon is personalized for human understanding: there are three principles—Trimurti; seven principles—Septimia; and nine principles—Nonimia.

Messengers and Religions

Septrionic followers believe that Eon, throughout all epochs of existence of the planet, sent messengers to different continents. They believe that all religions, whatever names by which they are called, when practiced with rectitude, are equally valid spiritual paths that lead to Eon. The doctrine sustains that all the founders of such religions were favorite sons sent by Eon to guide human beings in their spiritual evolution. Septrionism recognizes the supreme reality that there are two classes of religiosity: those who seek the light and practice goodness, and those who immerse themselves in obscurity and who practice only evil, inculcating hatred, division, and fratricidal violence. All human beings, whatever their race or creed, are sons and daughters of only one Creative Nature, which can be named by infinite denominations—and this does not alter or modify its unity. Rather, this reaffirms its universality and its greatness. Septrionic doctrine is conducive to harmonic and peaceful coexistence for all the believers of distinct spiritual paths.

In the Septrionic order, only the Eon of Eternal Intelligence is adored and venerated. Second, Septrionism honors and respects all the messengers of Eon without preference or competitiveness. All are one in the love of the Father Creator. For this reason, they invite believers of all religions of the world to their universal rites, where all unite as children of universal love in order to banish all vestiges of hatred. Members of the order express their love of all religions and to all human beings without distinction of creed, race, or social differences.

Shikry Gama is the spiritual guide for the Septrionics, and his teachings and precepts shape the Septrionic doctrine as compiled by Brother Claudio. The Divine conceded to the native peoples of the American continent a messenger of light, an Inca ruler called Man Ko Ka Li. He was entrusted to bring a spiritual path to native peoples of South America equal to that conceded to other messengers of light on other continents. The inhabitants of that continent have forgotten his existence.

The Soul and Reincarnation

Septrionics believe in the preexistence and postexistence of the soul. They believe that the idea of the soul (from the Greek *atma*) and spirit (from the Latin) refer to the same existent nature. They believe that after death, there is continuity of the psychic experiences held in life. Septrionics do not believe in death as such, but in the transition from physical life to the life of the spirit. After the corporal transition, we will continue the quality of ethical, moral, and spiritual life with the same attitudes that we held during our corporal existence.

Septrionics believe in *yuxtacarnación* (juxtacarnation): the spirit or the soul is juxtaposed to a carnal body. The spirit does not reside within the human body, but instead, it is united to it by a fluid electromagnetic canal of mutual induction. The incarnation of the human soul requires an embryonic period of thirty-five days to culminate the corporal symbiosis, which initiates the fetal period. The basic principle of reincarnation involves the notion that all human beings are incarnated spirits; thus we must know a natural or supernatural law that can impede the repetition of a phenomenon that has already been produced in the first place. Reincarnation or juxtaincarnation is the transition of successive lives that permits the spirit to seek its realization and spiritual evolution, to liberate itself from the domain of the body in order to return to the energetic dimension of its origin and to incarnate again to accomplish its existential mission.

The *transhabitual space* is a spiritual dimension destined to mitigate the physiological necessities that still underlie the consciousness of the late disincarnated spirits during a period of transformation of its psychic habits, until it is liberated from its bodily dependence.

A CONCISE HISTORY OF SEPTRIONISM

Here is a brief summation, then, of Septrionic history and beliefs.

- Claudio Cedeño (Shikry Gama) created a doctrine based on personal revelation, with his source of knowledge coming directly from the spiritual world in the astral plane.
- His purpose was to achieve coherence and unity between religious and moral values on the one hand and science on the other. The group's doctrines were viewed as harmonious with modern science and not in opposition to its methodologies and theories about the nature of reality.
- We can describe Septrionism as a contemporary mystical approach to self-knowledge and self-development, with emphasis on change. Personal knowledge of the spiritual world is primary. The goal is to control our instincts and passions. It sees as its role to provide a new view of the world and to delineate universal laws of causality. The doctrine questions the mission of human beings in society and their relationship to eternal forces. The primary focus of the doctrine is helping humankind to achieve spiritual peace and to overcome afflictions and tribulations.
- Other doctrinal fundamentals:

    Divinity is not viewed as a being, as in the Judeo-Christian system, but as the Eon of Eternal Intelligence. Divinity is a conjunct of creating, transforming, and balancing energies that govern by universal laws.

    Dual oppositions exist in nature, and Shikry Gama presents reasons and arguments for the existence of laws of oppositions and laws of constant transformation and transmutation. In fact, duality is a fundamental concept. Human beings, too, are dual in nature. Instinctive beings are contrasted negatively with volitional humans. The latter can achieve a superior destiny.

Human beings are historic beings in a socio-familiar nucleus. Each person's behavior constitutes an example and registry of the characteristics of the values that are demonstrated in our daily attitudes, which we pass on to our children.

Much of human tradition and misfortune derives from the domination of the instinctual part of human beings, which we gain from our genetic heredity. Until a time when individuals rationally use their intelligence, they will not be able to eliminate their conflicts and suffering.

Unlike many great world religions, Septrionism believes that human beings reward or punish themselves as a result of their actions. As in the Hindu system—but from a totally different perspective—reincarnation is the means by which occurs all that is conducive to spiritual evolution.

♦ Septrionic goal: dignifying of human beings in order to help them to understand the reality in which they live and to show them the reasons for the values that regulate their conduct in ethical and moral realms.

♦ Septrionism does not place in the individual the fear of an angry god who punishes those who lack knowledge of his designs and plans. Rather, Septrionism argues that human beings must observe some norms and reject others in order to harmonize their own interests in the hopes of living in peace and harmony with society. Septrionic philosophy and teachings do not invoke the fear of God to cause adherents to regulate their moral and ethical behavior. Septrionism sustains that it is an error to believe the idea of a punishing god.

♦ Science is not viewed as opposed to traditional religious criteria, although science in general has produced a weakening of people's faith and beliefs in a force that is superior: the Divine. This weakening of faith and belief has produced psychic instability in the individual.

Septrionism insists on demonstrating that the inherited ideas of the past have confused the individual of the twenty-first century, and these ideas continue to demonstrate that science is not opposed to Eon's nature. On the contrary, Septrionism affirms that science is the only rational way of explaining and understanding the nature of Eon's volition. Rather than showing that Eon is dead, Septrionism tries to help us realize that science, in fact, demonstrates the presence of God in all of nature's manifestations. The doctrine attempts to teach individuals why they have come to earth, why they suffer anguish, and what will happen to their being after physical death—in order to enable them to find in this process the security of knowing their Creator.

♦ Human beings are responsible for their own correct or incorrect behavior and must be conscious of it. As with other universalist creeds, Septrionism accepts followers from all religious affiliations as long as a sense of the Creator is acknowledged and honored. Adherents of Septrionism view much of the disharmony between distinct religions on earth as due to the ignorance, egoism, and power ambitions of their leaders. Religion, for Shikry Gama, is not a divine mandate, but a human spiritual need as human beings search to identify themselves with their Creator.

♦ Septrionism venerates only the Creator and not the various messengers or prophets who are found historically in different creeds. Within its rituals, Septrionism honors and authorizes the glorification of the messengers who gave rise to the different religions.

♦ The organization is eminently monotheistic. All earthly paths, creeds, and religions have one source of origin of their beliefs. Calling the Divine Energies the Trimurti (the Three), the Septimia (the Seven), and the Nonimia (the Nine), the name *Septrionism* derives from those forces, which have always existed and have been the components of energies that created the visible universe and the planet Earth.

Septrionic doctrine differentiates religion from mysticism. Through time, religion has been a revelation that human beings receive by the will and action of the Divine, which is manifested by means of teachings and commands that try to lead a confused humankind toward a sense of their own spirituality and a perfection of their own nature. Mysticism, on the other hand, is the need in human beings, through service, meditation, analysis, and perception of our cognitive intelligence, to clarify the laws of nature and to identify the presence of the Divine in the realm of the world. Human beings are taught to sublimate their spirit until they can obtain union with their causal essence. In contrast, the religious attitude is one in which human beings delegate willpower in the Divine as the cause and effect of their existence. According to the mystical attitude, we know that the presence of the Divine is in all things and in all actions. Humans try to discover the dynamic operation of these laws to find their own perfection and to offer themselves to the Creation as unconditional servants.

Is Septrionism a religion? It is certainly a mystical approach to life. Within it, we learn to know ourselves. With this knowledge, we can actively seek the sublimation of our spirit. The sublimation of the ego is important so that we can become elevated to divine grace. The soul or spirit of human beings is viewed not as immaterial, but material. Septrionism has drawn on other sources as well as inventing a series of techniques to aid in the development of the internal faculties of its followers. Both prophecy and out-of-body experiences facilitate people's means of achieving subjective experiences to verify the existence of the astral world.

The original name of the organization has caused confusion. It has been identified with Brahamanism of India and Lamaism of Tibet, which have been sources of information and theoretical concepts that have influenced Western civilization. The potential energies of Creation were personified in the Hindu religion as Brahma, Shiva, and Vishnu, which in summary is one part of the energy essence of what is called the Eon of Eternal Intelligence. In order to not be confused with religion, the name was changed from Brahamanism and Lamaism to Septrionism. Shikry Gama claims to have a direct connection to astral Brahamanism and Lamaism, which is totally different from the ideas of existing religions nowadays. All major religious figures—Jesus, Siddhartha, Krishna, Rama, Tao—are one single spiritual being who, according to the Divine Creator, Brahma, incarnated in distinct epochs to guide and bring the primary teaching for the spiritual necessities of the civilizations of their time.

There are many roads to enlightenment. One is a psychological and philosophical approach, and a second focuses on mystical techniques. The first path is found by means of study, seminars, and lectures for intellectual growth. Each of us who aspires to enlightenment must prioritize the objective to re-encounter ourselves; to discover where we come from and where we want to go; to know who we were, who we are, and who we will be eternally, according to Shikry Gama's writings. The second approach, called *psychonomics,* utilizes breathing and meditative techniques to awaken our faculties and to cultivate our spirituality. It is taught to most members of the Septrionic order.

Once men and women are accepted into the order, they move through a hierarchy in which they are expected to render service to humankind.

The most important ritual of Septrionic practice is the weekly silent meditation held each Tuesday from 8:00 P.M. to 9:00 P.M. During this time, in a ceremony called Introeonization, individuals attempt to put themselves in contact with the universe's eternal intelligence. Through meditation in this ceremony, Septrionic followers all over the globe create a powerful mental chain based on the ceremonial eonization of water, which each individual drinks at the end of the ceremony. The *aratri* (altar) consists of a wooden triangle with three tiers.

Septrionic Practice and Meditation

Meditation techniques include closing our eyes and waiting to receive the spiritual light of the Divine, which permits each of us to see with clarity our internal spiritual world. At the opening of the ceremony, one of the assistants approaches the vertex of the altar, pointing to the east, and solicits the presence of a spiritual custody for that vertex and, through him, the presence of the Omnipotent Trimurti Brahamanica and the Omnisapient Septimia. This first *triara* (triangle of the altar) can be lit either by an accepted member of the Septrionic Sacred Mystical Order or by a follower of any other religion. In this case, such a person must be familiar with Septrionic ritual. This first triara can be lit either by one individual or in *triada* (three different individuals in triangular formation) moving around the vertices with each person lighting one of the vertices.

The second triangle, raised above the first lit one, can be lit by a designated auxiliary official or an initiated servant, member of the triada. The third vertice can be lit only by the founder of Septrionism and by those who have been consecrated as an Eonté (officiant).

Prayers are recited, and in the third triangle the Omnipotent Trimurti Brahamanica is called upon. The same prayer of solicitation is recited by each celebrant. There are a series of ritual prayers and songs and then absolute silence that can differ in duration for the greater part of an hour, while each person meditates on his personal problems. After a time, the Eonté prepares a communal cup of the eonized water, which is drunk by all those present as a sign of spiritual identification and to receive the response of their prayers through the Divine fragrance that is condensed in the water.

Prayers are recited in a liturgical language that members must memorize. Within the organization, there are a group of Lamas who occupy a high status in the organization's spiritual hierarchy, The consecrated Lamas are not viewed as representing the Divine before human beings; rather, they are representatives of men and women before the Divine. The Septimia is visualized as vibratory energies of seven elements: harmony, cognition, chemistry/physics, economy, sanitation/health, animal/vegetable kingdom, and human relations. Within the liturgical language, they are given special spiritual names.

The altar symbols are derived from the representation of Trimurti,

Septimia, and Nonimia, which are the mysterious forces that constitute the essence of divine intelligence. The focus of Septrionic justice and equity is sustained by the law of cause and effect, in which all action has its logical consequence. All of life's circumstances are the consequence of our former actions. The only correct action is to wish well to others, because all evil that we wish upon others will rebound in evil upon ourselves. Silence activates thinking; therefore silence is viewed as the unique way in which human beings can communicate with the Divine.

Assistants, sympathizers, and members must enter the ceremonial area barefoot and without mundane objects to show their humility before their Creator. They are cautioned to avoid the ostentatious display of jewelry or fancy clothing. Members wear a sacred cloak for the ceremony in the color that is symbolic of their spirit guide and distinct mystical routes. These were made known to them when they first joined the order. It is also a symbol of submission and veneration.

The colors of participants' cloaks include blue for the followers of Christ; rose for those who follow Confucius; green for the followers of the Buddha; yellow for those who follow an ancient Inca ruler, Man Ko Ka Li; gray for the followers of Muhammad; dark red for those who follow Brahma; and an intense red ochre for those who follow Shikry Gama. Other philosophical routes are coded symbolically if there are followers in the order. The ceremonial cloaks are used by the Lamas as well as the members accepted in the order. During the meditation, eyes are kept closed in an attempt to perceive the spiritual light of the Eon of Eternal Intelligence, or the Divine. Closing the eyes allows us to see with clarity our internal spiritual world. During the silence, individuals are expected to analyze introspectively their tribulations, to identify them with their conscience through the help of divine light. After meditating on our problems and possible solutions, we must then also ask for help for others who are in similar circumstances and for those suffering from more diverse types of problems. Drinking the eonized water is a sign of solidarity and identification with the common cause of those gathered. Each of those present, if he wishes, drinks the eonized water.

The eonization of water is seen to be a metaphysical process in which the essential physical element of water in its saturated and condensed essence molds eonically and eonically incorporates the thought exhalations of those present as the vibratory forces of the Divine. The thought vibrations of those present synchronize with those of the Divine, and the two fuse, polarize, and precipitate metaphysical forces to help complete and realize desired goals. In many folklores of the world, water exposed to the sun or moon absorbs the medical energies of these bodies, and when given to humans to drink, produces curative effects. This phenomenon is similar to that described and sought after in the ceremony: water is an immanent element, which can absorb all electromagnetic energy.

Adherents follow with faith, a logic of the revelations in the person of Brother Claudio's writings of the doctrines of Shikry Gamy, which link cause and effect in terms of electromagnetic forces that operate on the material realm. Thus, human beings, through the special force of mental concentration, are believed to be able to infiltrate water by emanations and projections of electromagnetic energy from their own willpower and thoughts. This creates a state that consubstantiates with that of water. By means of the benevolent participation of the divine intelligence, there is an overflowing induction toward all those who drink the eonized water.

Septrionism has its headquarters in the district of Lurin, a small city one hour outside of Lima, Peru. The headquarters are close to a famous archaeological site, the Temple of the Moon (Pachacamac). There are several hundred members and centers in Peru, Spain, Bolivia, and Brazil. Since 1986, I have helped to establish a center in California, and the organization has been granted nonprofit status as a religious entity.

In chapter 6, we will turn to the concepts of destiny elaborated by Shikry Gama, which are in stark contrast to the reliance on chance as seen in Belen with the naipes fortune-telling cards.

6

SEPTRIONIC
CONCEPTS

Destiny, Personal Control,
and Poverty

Shikry Gama wrote in his unpublished writings that every time he reflects on destiny, he encounters contradictory arguments that are confusing. Clearly, this is a complex issue. "Every time we observe the creation of the worlds and the existence of all that surrounds us, we perceive with clarity that God, in Its infinite wisdom established an order with the purpose that all that is created is destined to carry out Its commands, Its will and Its desires."[1]

He deduces from this premise that everything is predetermined by Eon (God). Destiny, however, is not invariable but rather dual and in opposition, as well as harmonic, with its own nature. This is a natural law that governs us. The study of biological science allows us to understand the laws that preestablish and determine the destiny of genetics in all living species. At first blush, these arguments can be seen to be determinant, as if human beings don't have the right or the freedom to live their own lives. Some people might think that Septrionism says on the one hand that Eon predetermines everything and then argues on the other hand that we can modify destiny. Isn't that contradictory? It may seem so, but it isn't. Fundamental laws of the Septrionic cosmogony are that opposites and transformations occur.

Opponency, a word coined by Septrionic order, and transformation are fundamental laws of Septrionic cosmogony and are titled, together, the Law of Opponence and Transformation. The Law of Opponence is universal and establishes that all incidents of complementary forces in a point of energetic functional impact generate a third dual force that expands in mutual attraction and repulsion until a new point of probative impact is reached. In opponence, opposites do not negate or exclude each other. They only reject each other by the opposition of their causality. In opponence, the opposites are complemented, rather than contradicted. They are not more than two contrary aspects of the same reality (a dual unity).

Shikry Gama argues in his lectures that with the knowledge of these laws, we can perceive and understand that nothing is static, that nature is in constant transformation, and therefore everything becomes diversified. In this way, the appraisal allows us to perceive different aspects of reality at the same time, instead of allowing us to see only one part. Shikry Gama also wrote that even though it is certain that we have a genetic destiny predetermined by our genes, Eon has also granted individuals free will, so that if we have the will to change, we may stop being what we are (or what we are not), so that our different attitude changes our genetic destiny. In this manner, genetics polarize but do not determine our attitudes. In the Septrionic doctrine, free will has four steps that human beings take, consciously or unconsciously, in order to act: (1) wishing, (2) selecting, (3) deciding or choosing, and (4) acting. Shikry Gama's teachings on free will and causality instruct individuals to assume responsibility for their own destiny. The founder makes us aware that by our actions and choices we make, we indeed construct our own destiny, and we also continue to suffer the consequences of our actions.

Also part of the Septrionic teachings is that we can modify the causality of our destiny through our behavior. Contrary to what we sometimes conceive of as destiny—something beyond our will—in reality, destiny is only the causality of our actions. Given our genetics, our environment, and the motivations we encounter in life, we can vary and cause our behavior—and with it, our destiny—to diversify. All people can act within a great range of possibilities. Whatever we do, we will always be acting within the duality of preestablished destinies. In destiny, we foresee the possibility of modification. Our character authentically falls into line with that which is contained in our genetic code—which, in turn, is modified through interaction with our social and cultural environment.

If we lack positive values, virtues, and talents, and when our genetic inheritance and cultural environment are negative, the innermost self has the right and the duty to change, to find in what Shikry Gama calls the *di-authenticity* the realization of an authentic paradigm that marks our interactions as harmonic and compatible. Shikry Gama writes about three phenomena: (1) authenticity, (2) di-authenticity, and (3) inauthenticity. He differentiates the nature of human beings' authenticity and di-authenticity, which are opponent, and fundamental characteristics of human reality. Free will was given to us so that we human beings could, given the will to change, stop being pretenders. In this way, we present ourselves and invent personalities for ourselves that are not sincere. In Septrionic doctrine, there is a need for a di-authentic person, different from what we pretend to be, different from our authentic nature. Thus, *di-authentic* is defined as a diversity of attitudes in which we are different from our authentic phenotype. The authentic being is that which our phenotype preestablishes as the inheritance of the characteristics of our progenitors in our genetic code. Added to this are the environmental and cultural influences that we have incorporated during our lives.

A prime concept in Septrionism is that of free will, *libre albedrio*, which infuses human personality. Conscious or volitional use of free will allows us to repress some attitudes and liberate or forge ahead with others.

Fig. 1. Ceremony of Gratitude—opening of a vertex of the altar

Fig. 2. Ceremony of Gratitude—sharing eonized water

Fig. 3. Ceremony of Gratitude—opening of a vertex of the altar by Grand Lama Shikry Gam

Fig. 4. Ceremony of Gratitude—prayer to spiritual guides

Fig. 5. The Eonization ceremony

Fig. 6. Ceremony of Gratitude—offerings of aromas and food

Fig. 7. Listening to the motivation of the Eonte (priest)

Fig. 8. Ceremony in honor of the late Sister Pepita

Fig. 9. Ceremony of Missionary Initiation

Fig. 10. Ceremony of Gratitude

We are free to choose wisely and responsibly what we want to be. We therefore must look for our positive destiny. The concept of destiny in Septrionismo implies the possibility of modification. For the Septrionic, "to modify" means to request that the light of Eon illuminates our destiny, and at the same time we put ourselves at the disposal of the force of destiny.

THE SEPTRIONIC CONCEPT OF CONTROL (CONTROLARIDAD)

Shikry Gama argues that when we try to analyze the destiny of our existence, we usually symbolize it as a ship, which leaves from a point and moves through space and time toward a final destination. We start that trip through the corporeal existence of our birth, searching for our strong desires, life questions, and goals, which finally lead us, either before or with death, to the destiny that we trace ourselves.

As with all traveling ships, ours encounters obstacles, storms, dangers, and uncertainties. In order to surmount all these unknown factors, our vessel needs a good pilot who is able to control the ship in any of the situations that nature holds in store for us. A good steersman knows how and when to control the ship in any contingency, accelerating, slowing down, or stopping the journey altogether, depending on the need to avoid difficulties until we reach our final destiny. This metaphor means that we must be good pilots in our own lives. If we don't control the rudder of our lives, we run the risk of experiencing a multitude of vicissitudes, adversities, and tribulations.

Control is the key to making of our lives what we set out to have them become. In order for us to control our lives, we must know ourselves very well. We also must know the course of our activities and the environment in which we will move. Without this foreknowledge, we will know neither where to go nor how to avoid the dangers that life has in store for us. Septrionism calls this capacity to control our life the *gift of self-control*. This gift consists of having the willpower and the capacity to control our instincts, feelings, emotions, and reactions. Having this gift is the key to human relations. It allows us to obtain harmony in our family and social and work interactions and to succeed in our life goals. To develop this gift, we must assume a permanent critical attitude in our daily conduct. We must forever watch over our emotions, feelings, and resentments, repressing all reactions that could cause us adverse consequences. We must learn to choose wisely the forms of expression that we establish in our personal relations. We must learn to select the activities, friendships, and objectives that we ourselves propose.

Often we have to repress our emotional reactions, for there will be situations in which we will have to speed up necessary events to accomplish our goals. We must learn to control our natural instincts in order not to enslave ourselves to satisfying physical or spiritual pleasures. We must learn to know when to say yes and when to say no. When we accept what we should reject or reject what we should accept, we experience confusion and conflicts in our interactions. We must learn to infer what is convenient and what is not. We must recognize our human weaknesses and not fall into the erroneous thinking that what has happened to others will not happen to us. Emotionality usually makes us react to any external stimulus or family experience. We often react vehemently and impulsively and express our sympathies or antipathies without reflecting or anticipating the consequences of our opinions and attitudes. We make mistakes, we are imprudent and impertinent, and we commit offenses that inevitably produce all kinds of tribulations.

To control our emotional reactions is a difficult art to exercise, but as we learn it, we make of our lives a permanent world of realization and achievements. We must learn to control our gestures, the tone of our voice, the words that we choose, the glances and emotional reactions that we express. We must control our tongue so that we speak only when it is indispensable to do so and are quiet when it is necessary not to be disloyal or indiscreet. We must learn to control our impulses, to know what things we can do, and what things we don't even have to try to do. We must learn to control our desires and fears in order to make the correct decisions. Such control allows us to overcome obstacles, to solve problematic situations, and to surmount the faintheartedness that frustrates our lives until we find the motivations that give us a reason to be, to exist, and to do all those things that we yearn to do in order to rid ourselves of our anguish and fears.

Controlling our emotional reactions is an aspiration that must permanently impel our will to change and desire to develop the gift of self-control. Those of us who are able to have this mental attitude will be able to manage life and lead destiny toward the goals to which we aspire. When we don't have the knowledge of what is correct as opposed to what is incorrect, when we cannot differentiate reality from utopian idealism, we will not be able to avoid becoming victims of errors, mistakes, and failures, and we will fall into the anarchy of values that is so common in our society.

Shikry Gama argues that we human beings have lost control of our destiny. We have lost the objectivity of our goals. We have lost the correct knowledge of the values and virtues that we should practice in order to achieve our aspirations. Many of us don't even know what we want from life or to what we want to dedicate ourselves. Disorder, anarchy, and social chaos force our world to convulse and agonize in all strata of existence. The need to reflect and to develop the gift of self-control is crucial. Never forget, writes Shikry Gama, that our destiny depends on our control of ourselves, because we are only what we do—not what we pretend to be.

POVERTY

In thinking about our destiny and how to manage it in a positive way, we must look at poverty itself. Examining poverty is necessary, for, as I have argued, the culture of poverty has been responsible—for instance, among both men and women in Belen—for the widespread dependence on chance, and, specifically, the use of such fortune-telling devices as the naipes to predict the future. In this context, we can look at the California lottery, for example. Perhaps there is some way to measure percentages of people with incomes below the national average in the interest of seeing if this is the population most likely to buy lottery tickets. When I last looked, the odds of winning a jackpot in the California lottery were fourteen million to one. Nonetheless, I know a young woman, a classmate of my daughter in high school, who was one of the lucky winners. Psychologists love this kind of positive reinforcement: If what's-her-name won the lottery, why not me? A person might say, remembering the vague promises and forgetting the prophecies that didn't materialize: if Maria in Belen had her fortune told successfully, why not me?

Shikry Gama writes about poverty and the impact it has on our way of seeing, the way we view the world. Living as he does in an underdeveloped nation, Peru, in a country with a very high percentage of practicing Catholics, he turns to the history of poverty to unravel the causes of this adversity. He sees the difference between developed and underdeveloped countries in terms of the influence of religion and its effect on politics, thinking, and attitudes.

Historically, we can focus on religious leaders who caused many problems for humanity. Shikry Gama cites the dogmatic zeal and fervor of the early Catholic church leaders, who tried to follow what they thought was the will of Jehovah as well as what Jesus said to his disciples. They did not dare to vary the texts of the Judaic-Christian religions, even if they understood that there were errors in those texts. Many of the teachings were ambiguous. As Pope John Paul II proposed in his encyclical *Tertio Milenium Adviente,* there is an unmet need to rectify errors and sins. Pope John Paul II, in the celebration of his Jubilee, said: "The Church even being holy through its incorporation in Christ does not tire of performing penance. The church always recognizes in front of men and women the sinful sons. It affirms the respect of *lumen gentium.* The Church embraces in its bosom sinners, it is both sacred and always in need of purification. It seeks without ending conversion and renewal."[2] This did not always occur historically, as we will see.

What Shikry Gama states in his writings is that countries that do not achieve development can be seen as subject to the biblical prohibition, attributed to God, that states that Adam and Eve must not eat from the Tree of Knowledge. This prohibition has disastrous consequences for the socioeconomic future of humanity. Due to a predetermined disobedience of that mandate, Adam and Eve were expelled from earthly paradise and sentenced to live by the sweat of their brow. Knowledge and labor were inexplicably repudiated in the Bible.

Organized religion turned this allegory into original sin, thereby sentencing humanity to suffer collectively a guilt complex based only on this doctrine. The results have been a tremendous fear for all cognitive input and a subliminal feeling of repudiation of knowledge. Over the last twenty centuries, this repudiation sentenced Christian believers to ignorance and poverty within Christianity. Apparently, the authors of that biblical passage naively thought that God the Father did not wish human beings to have knowledge of his psychophysical nature or of the laws of survival or that human beings could acquire the knowledge that is necessary to transform their environment in order to preserve equilibrium and the life that they had been granted. This has created a culture of dependence.

There is a paradox in understanding and interpreting the will and love of the principle of divine all-knowingness. To many, this appears to be the will of the principle of chaos. There is no doubt that those human beings who edited the biblical history of the fall from grace were confused, which led them to the error of imposing obedience to everything that seems to be contrary to God's purpose.

At present, all humanity understands that work is the prayer that most pleases God—and even more so if it is work that benefits our fellow human beings. Yet without knowledge, it is not possible to give to work the added value of utility, of savings, and of capitalization. Without knowledge, it will never be possible to surmount poverty or the adversities of life. It is a serious theological error to conceive of a God who has the same weaknesses as human beings—and thus a God who allows himself to be dragged down by anger, denial of love, and solidarity among individuals and social groups. God had to have this love toward solidarity with his Creation. In an evil manner, this sentences all of humanity to live in ignorance and poverty.

For inscrutable reasons, the church leaders assumed for themselves the historical mission to teach their flocks to bear the adversity of poverty. History is populated with testimonies, statements, and denunciations against religion and priests for not having solved the problem of poverty.

These priests, lost by the complexity of factors that prevented them from solving humanity's inequality, opted to console the poor with litanies such as, we can die of hunger and suffering in this valley of tears, but in heaven, next to God, the beneficent sun will caress our brow, and the Milky Way will serve us as a carpet. We will not need to eat. However, we will have the immense joy in our revenge of hearing tyrants gnawed by torment and hunger for centuries and centuries to come.

To strengthen the hope of the consolation offered by priests for all the frustrations, tribulations, and miseries of the poor, the church decided to attribute to God the will of justice after death. This was to compensate the poor, who were to be repaid in Paradise after they died.

Some of these religious clergy managed to live sanctified lives by dedicating themselves to carrying out vows of poverty in an exemplary manner. Rather than eradicating poverty, however, they increased its presence in those populations already mired in it.

Historically, it is interesting to note that Catholic believers were always economically underdeveloped, while the most economically developed peoples have been Protestants. This contrast is not to attribute blame but instead is noted to try to discover what preestablished attitudes resulted in these lamentable differences. Apparently, the inspiration that motivated those who looked to overcome spiritual tribulations and economic deficiencies amounted to the spiritual renunciation of the wealth of the physical world. Personal attitudes could be cited to explain these differences, and this has been studied in many scholarly works on Protestantism and the rise of capitalism.[3] This was not always illuminated by the light of understanding that common men had to overcome their own adversities.

Shikry Gama quotes Jesus's words in the Bible: "It is easier for a camel to pass through the eye of a needle than for a rich man to pass through the door of my father's kingdom" (Matthew 19:24). He notes that to attribute an insidious and unjust sentence to the son of God the Father exemplified an abominable hatred of the rich by Christianity—yet we note that Jesus was protected by a rich man, Joseph of Arimathea.

The history of Western society would have been different if this passage expressed: "It is easier for a camel to pass through the eye of a needle than a greedy man to pass through the doors of my father's kingdom." Indeed, a difference exists between avarice and generosity, just as there exists a difference between hell and heaven.

The Christian world was contaminated by resentments and great hatreds of the rich, and erroneously inculcated the repudiation of those who practiced the exemplary talents that Jesus himself taught. Manual labor was despised until, ironically, it provoked social reactions and awakened resentments against religion. This propitiated the idea that religion was the opium of the masses. The priesthood was indifferent and lived a life of luxury and comfort without concerning itself with the misery and adversities of the people.

It has also been suggested that Jesus said: "Blessed are the poor of spirit because they will inherit the kingdom of heaven." It is evident in a figurative sense that the "poor of spirit" refers to the concept of virtuous humility, with very few spiritual people able to set an example. The solemn vows of poverty that religious people take should not be confused with the deprivation of the needy. This first type of poverty is a state of voluntary abdication of everything that we own and all that pride can judge necessary to demonstrate to God the renunciation of worldly physical goods.

It is comprehensible to admit that poverty understood as a lack of values and virtues could deserve God's mercy and forgiveness. Poverty, however, does not suppose equality of virtues and the merits that were required for us to deserve to enter the kingdom of heaven. Poverty accepted with patience, resignation, and dignity becomes humility and is pleasing to God. Jesus himself glorified the humble, both rich and poor, because there is no doubt that heaven must and should comprise those who are humble and virtuous and who renounce all things material in order to offer up their lives to God.

There are those who decide on a priestly service. Yet in the economic poverty of humanity, there is not only voluntary renunciation. There is also shameful economic deprivation, which goes against human dignity. Such deprivation provokes ever more desperate and excessive demand by the poor regarding everything that they lack.

The term *poverty* is a noun that denotes destitution, misery, absolute necessity, shortage, and lack of the indispensable necessary to sustain life. The causes of poverty can be neurological dysfunction, cognitive and sensory limitations, bad habits, traumas and complexes, deficiencies in human education, absence of ideas and ingenuity, ignorance or deficiency of virtues and talents, lack of opportunities, or lack of love in carrying out duties.

The concept of *poverty* exclusively refers to the lack of physical goods, while the concept of *humility* exalts the exercise of a virtue consisting of an individual knowing his own defects and errors without being ostentatious or boasting about the good qualities or the virtuous actions that he performs. Such a person considers performing virtuous acts as a duty and his good qualities as a gift of nature or the hand of God. Thus, humility has nothing to do with the possession or lack of physical goods. Rich and poor men can be virtuous or depraved, and as such, rich men and poor men can also be humble.

Poverty is a condition that all human beings must take responsibility for to help eradicate in society. The rich along the way have been blamed exclusively as being the cause of poverty and underdevelopment.[4] This is truly unjust and far from the truth, according to Shikry Gama. Who is really the guilty party in this situation? Is it not perhaps the responsibility of those who lack something and who need to seek out the necessary judicious actions required to solve their own problems?

This responsibility is implicitly suggested in another statement attributed to Jesus: "Seek and you will find" (Matthew 7:7–8). It is evident that the person who does not look to solve his lack of necessities will not find the solution to this lack. The seeker is the needy one, and he makes an error of negligence when he waits for a generous donor to solve his lack through the giving of alms (or, as argued in this book, through dependence on the naipes fortune-telling cards). This error has led the poor to believe that begging will solve their problems and that not only the rich but also God has a duty to give them alms in abundance. They believe, therefore, that in this way they can solve their lack of necessities of survival.

We need not seek out discourse to see that those peoples and countries that want to be rich practice the principles of diligence and labor and become part of developed communities. Some were ambiguously taught: be negligent and lazy if you want to have the virtue of poverty— that the kingdom of God will be for the poor of spirit who end up becoming the flag carriers of underdevelopment.

Historically, the Protestants made the love of work and productivity into charitable virtues, which converted them into generous and untiring people who always helped and who continue to help those who made of poverty a false virtue. Theologians blamed others for what never was more than their own responsibility. The reasons that motivated theologians' dialectical thought are unfathomable, but they caused the poor to learn to live off begging for alms given to them by generous people. As time passes, the errors committed have become clear. Shikry Gama is hopeful that shedding light on the causes of this predicament will allow us to overcome these situations in order to see progress and well-being in underdeveloped countries.

The church must renew its efforts to fulfill the responsibility of those who assumed in the past the mission to fight poverty with teachings, discipline, and the practice of virtues. These can transform the psychosomatic cause of the needy's ignorance, negligence, and indolence. Correcting past errors will help the disadvantaged to climb out of poverty and underdevelopment.

7

FATE, FORTUNE, AND MYSTICISM

A Clearer View

What started out as an inquiry into fortune-telling in a Peruvian Amazon slum has become what may be called the "deep structure" of this divination technique and, eventually, an attempt to understand this effort at predicting destiny. Our journey has brought us to examine the teachings of a Peruvian mystical organization that looks at destiny in a distinctive manner. I am struck by how rich the Peruvian landscape is—giving rise to diverse ways of understanding human behavior: on the one hand, a transplanted (perhaps European) system of divination with probable Asian and Egyptian origins, and on the other, a relatively new spiritualist mystical religion.

Though for some, reading the naipes may appear as fun and games, for peasant people in Belen it is hardly irrelevant to their sad lives of privation and suffering. For me, the experiences of working with the poor people of Belen and of learning about and participating in the Septrionic rituals has been extraordinary. My personal experiences have been outside the range of that which we regard as ordinary. As a fortune-teller, I participated in social and ritual performances in which social realities were generated for my clients and I gained insight into their culture, stressors, and aspirations. I had the opportunity to enter an alternate way of perceiving, experiencing, and interpreting reality. My normal way of processing and classifying information was challenged. Certainly, I had an interest in parapsychology, but nothing to "write home about." I tried to understand parapsychology from a rational point of view, and in the 1970s I actually organized symposia in adult educational units on anthropology and the paranormal at the University of California at Berkeley, Los Angeles, and Irvine. Then, in Peru, I found that I was a conduit for my clients in the Iquitos slum—an agent to predict their future and confirm or deny their aspirations and hopes. I had no choice but to take seriously the extraordinary experiences of my informants, and in chapter 4, I examined a number of different explanations of the successes and failures of this technique. I also learned a great deal about healers whose job it was to be omnipotent. Using the naipes allowed them to appear all-powerful and all-knowing, as well as to learn about their clients' lives and incorporate the emotional expressiveness of their clients into their visionary outputs with the ayahuasca hallucinogenic potion.

SIMILARITIES AND DIFFERENCES BETWEEN NAIPES FORTUNE-TELLING AND SEPTRIONIC MYSTICISM

In this text are included two very disparate attempts to understand our destiny: the fortune-telling naipes cards and the Sacred Mystical Order of Septrionism. Yet for all the differences between these two, there are also similarities. In both systems, free will is at play. An individual in Peru can choose to have her fortune told or attend a Tuesday night meditation ceremony. The reputation of a curioso and the founder of Septrionism are both typically established by word of mouth. There is no advertising, although Septrionism does have a website* and is perhaps

---

*www.septrionismo.com

more interesting to urban, middle-class individuals than to farmers. But differences prevail. The curioso basically has a business endeavor: to obtain funds for his presumed special knowledge. The founder of the Septrionic order is part of a hierarchy of adherents who give service to the organization and who promulgate an important doctrine to interested individuals. Thus, the two exemplify individual activity versus group organization.

Differences do not stop there. The meaning of the naipes typically is known only to the curioso in Iquitos. In contrast, the doctrine of Septrionism is written and available in pamphlet form. It can be purchased by interested parties and is available to the reading public for a token cost of less than one dollar. The focus is on study and discussion groups. The individual who seeks out the curioso is a client, but the individual who attends meditation and visits the Septrionic headquarters near Lima is involved in ongoing personal transformation. The curioso's client generally has his fortune told one or two times at important life junctions, but an individual may have an ongoing devotion to the Septrionic order. The client interacts only with the curioso without any continuity or follow-up, but the Septrionic members interact with one another within a hierarchy and communicate frequently with one another and the founder.

In the realm of similarities, both the curioso and the founder of Septrionism claim knowledge from other realms via revelation, and both individuals are seen by their public as exceptionally talented people. Yet though the card reading of the naipes is a service given often at a high cost, membership in the Sacred Mystical Order of Septrionism includes tithes for members according to their ability to pay, similar to Christian churches around the world—but access is not limited if an individual does not tithe.

With the naipes, there are egocentric outcomes. The client asks himself: What does this reading do for me with regard to money, love, success, and so forth? Yet the ritual activities of Septrionism, such as meditation, reflection, study of doctrine, and discussion groups, help us to find our mission in life and help us to help establish and maintain moral and social values. Though the naipes client is passive, the Septrionic member is actively involved in prayer and reflection. The Septrionic member has bestowed upon himself a spiritual guide from which to follow and learn, but the naipes client goes through life on his own.

Both systems speak to the issue of our destiny. We passively accept the reading given or, in Septrionism, we learn to control our destiny. The naipes are part of an oral tradition—that is, fortune-telling with the naipes depends on word of mouth as the mechanism to spread the word. The Septrionic creed, however, is written and promulgated in a philosophical format presented in polished Spanish. With regard to self-control, if a client dislikes his fortune, some curiosos will return the fee and thus negate the outcome, in a kind of magical purchase. If the Septrionic member or follower is dissatisfied, the door is open for him to leave, just as it is open to him to enter the Septrionic temple.

This book presents the structural differences between two ways in which destiny is sought—the naipes on the one hand, and the Septrionic Mystical Order on the other—and both point out the ways in which human beings deal with the concept of destiny.

CONCLUSION

When I began to work with Septrionism in the late 1970s, I saw destiny in a different light. The weekly meditation sessions were unlike anything I had experienced in my life. One time, while sitting at a table and having coffee after the meditation, I touched Brother Claudio's hand as the sugar was being passed, and I almost fell off the chair to the floor as the result of an energy current that was indescribable. My husband and I work very hard at translating Septrionic doctrine from Spanish to English as best we can in expectation of future publications of the doctrine and the growth of the organization.*

As an anthropologist, I must address the question of the cross-cultural encounter and the changes I experienced. Psychologists worry about bias in their studies and therefore distance themselves carefully from their subjects. The experiences I had as a fortune-telling anthropologist may have been ordinary for the clients, but they were not so for me. I took the trouble to learn a code of communication in order to relate better to the people of Belen. I turned to science to make the data respectable. I compared responses to the three questions clients asked of the cards to themes I obtained from a respected psychological test, the

---

*The author takes responsibility for any errors in the Septrionic translations from Spanish to English.

TAT. I was able to inhabit the world of the river's-edge farmers in Belen through immersion with the naipes.

I was introduced to Septrionism through don Hilde, an ayahuasca healer with whom I worked in Pucallpa. In the United States, after my time in Belen, I learned how to be in control of my own destiny without recourse to fortune-telling cards, and I never used the cards irreverently in social settings. With Septrionic doctrine, however, I accept all accusations of bias and personal interest and expect to play a future role in bringing to light these metaphysical teachings.

NOTES

INTRODUCTION. FORTUNE-TELLING CARDS, MYSTICAL REFLECTION IN PERU

1. David Young and Jean-Guy Goulet, *Being Changed by Cross-cultural Encounters: The Anthropology of Extraordinary Experience* (Peterborough, Ontario: Broadview Press, 1994).

CHAPTER 1. THE HISTORY AND THE STRUCTURE OF THE NAIPES

1. Marlene Dobkin de Rios, "La Cultura de la Pobreza y la Magia de Amor: Un Sindrome Urbano en la Selva Peruana," *America Indigena* 29, no. 1 (January 1969): 3–16.
2. Corrine Kenner, *Simple Fortune-telling with Tarot Cards* (Woobury, Minn.: Llewellyn, 2007).
3. Marlene Dobkin de Rios, "La Cultura de la Pobreza y la Magia de Amor: Un Sindrome Urbano en la Selva Peruana," 3–16.

CHAPTER 3. BELEN: THE CULTURE OF POVERTY, THE NAIPES, AND LOVE MAGIC

1. Marlene Dobkin de Rios, *Visionary Vine: Hallucinogenic Healing in the Peruvian Amazon* (San Francisco: Chandler Publishing Co., 1972).
2. Enrique Grajeda, *Estuio Socio-economico de la Realidad e la Barriada de Belen* (Iquitos, Peru: Universidad Nacional e la Amazonia Peruana. Facultad de

Ciencias y Humaniaes, 1966); Jesus Oviedo et. al., *Estudio Sccio-economico de la Barriada el Puerto de Belen de la Ciudad de Iquitos* (Lima, Peru: Escuela de Servicio Social, 1964); Frits Wils, *Estudio Social sobre Belen, Iquitos* (Lima, Peru: Centro de Investigaciones Sociales, Económicas, Polticas y Anthropólogicas, 1967).

CHAPTER 4. MARLENE, THE FORTUNE-TELLER: SEEING MAGIC FROM THE INSIDE

1. Marlene Dobkin de Rios, "La Cultura de la Pobreza y la Magia de Amor: Un Sindrome Urbano en la Selva Peruana."
2. Daniel Kahneman and Gary Klein, "Conditions for Intuitive Expertise. A Failure to Disagree," *American Psychologist* 64, no. 6 (2008): 515–26.
3. Paul Ekman, *Emotions Revealed* (New York: Henry Holt and Co., 2003).
4. Randolph Nesse et. al. "Evolution, Emotions, and Emotional Disorders," *American Psychologist* 64, no. 2 (2009): 129–39.
5. Paul Ekman and Richard Davis, *The Nature of Emotions: Fundamental Questions* (New York: Oxford Press, 1944).
6. H. J. Eysenck, *Encyclopedia of Psychology,* vol. 2 (Bungay. Suffolk, England: Fontana, 1975), 1077.
7. John Schumaker, *Human Suggestibility. Advances in Theory, Research and Application* (New York: Routledge, 1991).

CHAPTER 5. THE SACRED MYSTICAL ORDER OF SEPTRIONISM: A PERUVIAN SPIRITUALIST RELIGION

1. Kenneth Wapnack, "Mysticism and Schizophrenia," *Journal of Transpersonal Psychology* 1, no. 2 (1969): 79–86.
2. Walter Terence Stace, *Mysticism and Philosophy* (Los Angeles: Tarcher, 1960).
3. Jean-Pierre Valla, *Mysticism Proceedings of the International Conference on Shamanism,* Ruth-Inge Heinze, ed. (Berkeley: Center for South and Southeast Studies, University of California, 1984).
4. David Hay and Ann Morrissey, "Secular Society, Religious Meanings: A Contemporary Paradox," *Review of Religious Research* 26, no. 3 (1985): 213–27.

5. Paul Heelas, *The New Age Movement* (Cambridge: Blackwell, 1996.)

6. David Lukoff et al., "Psychoactive Substances and Transpersonal States," *Journal of Transpersonal Psychology* 22, no. 2 (1990): 107–48.

7. Arthur Deikman, "Two Halves of the Brain," Phillip Lee, ed., *Symposium on Consciousness* (New York: Viking Press, 1976).

8. June Macklin, "Belief, Ritual and Healing: New England Spiritualism and Mexican American Spiritism Compared," I. Zaretsky and M. Leon, eds., *Religious Movements in Contemporary America* (Princeton, N.J.: Princeton University Press, 1974).

9. Joan Koss, "The Therapist-Spiritist Training Project in Puerto Rico: An Experiment to Relate the Traditional Healing System to the Public Health System," *Social Science and Medicine* 14B (1980): 373–410.

10. Sidney Greenfield, "Our Science Is Better than Yours: Two Decades of Data on Patients Treated by a Kardecist-Spiritist Healing Group in Rio Grande o Sul," *Anthropology of Consciousness* 20, no. 2 (2009): 101–10.

11. Elaine Pagels, *The Gnostic Gospels* (New York: Random House, 1979).

CHAPTER 6. SEPTRIONIC CONCEPTS: DESTINY, PERSONAL CONTROL, AND POVERTY

1. Shikry Gama, unpublished manuscript.

2. John Paul II, Jubilee quote.

3. Max Weber, *Protestantism and the Spirit of Capitalism* (New York/ Ontario: McMaster University Archive for the History of Economic Thought, 1905).

4. Frantz Fanon, *The Wretched of the Earth* (London: Penguin, 1969).

GLOSSARY

amor cochinado   Piggy love, caused by witchcraft hexes that result in a romantic union between a man and a woman

aratri   The Septrionic altar of service, offerings, and dedicated consecration to the Trimurti, the Septimia, and the Nonimia, which are the energetic principles that shape the essence of the Eon of Internal Intelligence

ayahuasca   A plant hallucinogen, *Banisteriopsis* sp.

ayahuasquero   A man who administers ayahuasca to his clients

baraja española   Spanish deck of cards

Beleño   Resident of the slum Belen, in Iquitos

Brujo(a)   Witch who uses hexes to harm enemies

caballo   Corresponds to the Queen in a deck of Western playing cards

cholo   An individual whose roots are Native American, and European, who is influenced by the national culture, speaks Spanish and is a Christian. The cholo continues to hold magical beliefs and rituals corresponding to his aboriginal roots.

curioso (a)   Man or woman who has some metaphysical skill such as reading the fortune-telling cards

daño   An illness caused by witchcraft

despecho   The malice an individual harbors toward another, causing him to seek out a witch to harm his enemy

Lo Dios   Septrionic term translated as the Divine

mal de ojo   Illness called "evil eye bewitchment"

mestizo(a)   Latin American man or woman whose heritage is both Native American and European

minga   Cooperative work group (e.g., which may repair a bridge in Belen)

naipes   A deck of playing cards with a long history. The naipes probably originated in Asia, were transported via India and probably Egypt to Europe, and then made their way to Latin America.

pulsario   An anxiety illness often attacking women

pusanga   A potion for love magic

rematista   An individual who resells produce in city markets such as Belen's for a small profit

regaton   Men who have launches and travel river systems bartering crops and manufactured goods to peasantry

sanitario   Men trained in the army as paramedics

San Pedro   A mescaline cactus used in folk healing in north coastal Peru

Septrionism   A mystical religious group headquartered near Lima, Peru

Sota   Corresponds to the Jack in a deck of Western playing cards

susto   Fright illness encountered in Peru with violent impression of fear

triada   Servants in charge of the ceremonial rites in Septrionismo, including *adicto, adepto,* and *vigilante*

Trimurti   Composed of three energetic principles: Brahama (energetic principle of creation); Vishnu (energetic principle of transformation); Shiva (energetic principle of equilibrium)

BIBLIOGRAPHY

Anonymous. *Cartomancia y Quiromancia. Adivincion del Presente y Porvenir por Medio de la Baraja Española.* Lima, Peru: Importadora y Distribuidora Rivera, n.d. (Originally published in 1864.)

Anonymous. *La Magia Blanca, Secreta y Adivinatoria.* Mexico: n.p., 1957.

Anonymous. *La Magia Negra y Arte Adivinatoria.* Mexico: n.p., n.d.

Anonymous. *La Magia Roja.* Mexico: n.p., 1957.

Anonymous. *La Magia Verde o Amorosa.* Mexico: n.p., 1957.

Boiteau d'Ambly, D. *Les Cartes a Jouer et la Cartomancie.* Paris: Hachette, 1854.

Court de Gebelin, M. *Monde Primitif, Analyse et Comparé avec le Monde Moderne,* vol. 8. Paris: Durand, 1781.

Deikman, Arthur. "Two Halves of the Brain." *Symposium on Consciousness.* Edited by Phillip Lee. New York: Viking Press, 1976.

de la Vega, Garcilaso. *The Royal Commentaries of the Incas.* Translated by Marie Jolas. New York: Orion, 1957.

Dobkin de Rios, Marlene. "A Note on the Use of Ethno-Tests and Western Projective Tests in a Peruvian Amazon Slum." *Human Organization* 30 (1971): 189–94.

———. "Curanderismo con la Soga Alucinogena (Ayahuasca) en la Selva Perúana." *América Indígena* 31, no. 3 (1971): 571–91.

———. "Fortune's Malice: Divination, Psychotherapy and Folk Medicine in Peru." *Journal of American Folklore* 82, no. 324 (1969): 38–41.

———. "La Cultura de la Pobreza y la Magia de Amor; un Síndrome Urbano en la Selva Perúana." *America Indigena* 29, no. 1 (January 1969): 3–16.

———. *Visionary Vine: Hallucinogenic Healing in the Peruvian Amazon.* San

Francisco: Chandler Publishing Co., 1972. (Reprinted by Prospect Heights, Ill.: Waveland Press, 1984).

Ekman, Paul. *Emotions Revealed.* New York: Henry Holt and Co., 2003.

Eysenck, H. J. *Encyclopedia of Psychology,* vol. 2. Bungay, Suffolk, England: Fontana, 1975.

Fanon, Frantz. *The Wretched of the Earth.* London: Penguin, 1969.

Gehricke, Jean, et al. "Smoking to Self-Medicate Attentional and Emotional Dysfunctions." *Nicotine and Tobacco Research* 9, no. 4 (2007): 523–36.

Grajeda, Enrique. *Estudio Socio-economico de la Realidad de la Barriada de Belen.* Universidad Nacional de la Amazonia Peruana. Facultad de Ciencias y Humanidades. Iquitos, Peru, 1966.

Greenfield, Sidney. "Our Science Is Better than Yours: Two Decades of Data on Patients Treated by a Kardecist-Spiritist Healing Group in Rio Grande do Sul." *Anthropology of Consciousness* 20 (2009): 2101–110.

Group for the Advancement of Psychiatry. *Mysticism: Spiritual Quest or Psychic Disorder?* Washington, D.C.: American Psychiatric Association. Committee on Psychiatry and Religion, 1976.

Hay, David, and Ann Morrissey. "Secular Society, Religious Meanings. A Contemporary Paradox." *Review of Religious Research* 26, no. 3 (1985): 213–27.

Heelas, Paul. *The New Age Movement.* Cambridge, Mass.: Blackwell, 1996.

Kahneman, Daniel, and Gary Klein. "Conditions for Intuitive Expertise. A Failure to Disagree." *American Psychologist* 64, no. 6 (2008): 515–26.

Kardec, Allan. *Spiritualist Philosophy. The Spirit's Book.* London: Ayre Publishing Co., 1976. (Originally published in 1893.)

Kenner, Corrine. *Simple Fortunetelling with Tarot Cards.* Woodbury, Minn.: Llewellyn Publications, 2007.

Koss, Joan. "The Therapist-Spiritist Training Project in Puerto Rico: An Experiment to Relate the Traditional Healing System to the Public Health System." *Social Science and Medicine* 14B (1980): 373–410.

Kroeber, Alfred. *Anthropology.* New York. Harcourt, Brace, and Co., 1923.

LeNormand, Madame Marie. *Arte de Echar las Cartas.* Mexico: n.p., n.d.

Levi, Eliphas. *Les Mysteres de la Kabbale.* Paris: Nourry, 1920.

Lewis, Oscar. *La Vida: A Puerto Rican Family in the Culture of Poverty—In San Juan and New York.* New York: Random House, 1966.

Lukoff, David, et al. "Psychoactive Substances and Transpersonal States." *Journal of Transpersonal Psychology* 22, no. 2 (1990): 107–48.

Macklin, June. "Belief, Ritual and Healing: New England Spiritualism and Mexican American Spiritism Compared." *Religious Movements in Contemporary America*. Edited by I. Zaretsky and M. Leon. Princeton: Princeton University Press, 1974.

Nesse, Randolph M., and Phoebe C. Ellsworth. "Evolution, Emotions, and Emotional Disorders." *American Psychologist* 64, no. 2 (2009): 129–39.

Oviedo, Jesus, et. al. *Estudio Socio-economico de la Barriada el Puerto de Belen de la Ciudad de Iquitos.* Lima, Peru: Escuela de Servicio Social, 1964.

Pagels, Elaine. *The Gnostic Gospels.* New York: Random House, 1979.

Papus. *Traite Methodique de Science Occulte,* 8 vols. Paris: J. B. Baillière et Fils, 1891.

Rhue, Judith W., Steven Jay Lynn, and Irvine Kisch, eds. *Handbook of Clinical Hypnosis.* Washington, D.C.: American Psychological Association, 1993.

Rumrill, Roger. *La Amazonia Peruana: La Ultima Renta Estrategica del Peru en el Siglo XXI o La Tierra Prometida.* Programa de las Naciones Unidas para el Desarrollo (PNUD). Lima, Peru: Fimart Editorial, 2008.

Schumaker, John. *Human Suggestibility. Advances in Theory, Research and Application.* New York: Routledge, 1991.

Segura, Manuel, and Helena Sanjaman. *Cartomancia.* Barcelona: n.p., 1956.

Silva, Max. "El Curanderismo en Lima." *Revista de Ciencias Psicologicas y Neurologicas* 2, no. 1 (1965): 16–49.

Simon, A. "What Is an Explanation of Behavior?" *Psychological Sciences* 3 (1992): 150–61.

Simon, H. A. "A Mechanism for Social Selection and Successful Altruism." *Science* 250 (1990): 1665–68.

Singer, Samuel W. *Researches into the History of Playing Cards.* London: T. Bensley and Son, 1816.

Spence, Lewis. *An Encyclopedia of Occultism.* London: George Routledge and Sons, Ltd., 1920.

Valla, Jean-Pierre. *Mysticism.* Edited by Ruth-Inge Heinze. Proceedings of the International Conference on Shamanism. Center for South and Southeast Asian Studies. Berkeley: University of California, 1984.

Van Rijnberg, G. *Le Tarot: Histoire, Iconographie, Esoterisme.* Lyon: Paul Derain, 1947.

Wapnack, Kenneth. "Mysticism and Schizophrenia," *Journal of Transpersonal Psychology* 1, no. 2 (1969): 79–86.

Weber, Max. *Protestantism and the Spirit of Capitalism*. New York: McMaster University Archive for the History of Economic Thought. Ontario, Canada, 1905.

Wils, Frits. *Estudio Social sobre Belen, Iquitos*. Centro de Investigaciones Sociales, Económicas, Polticas y Anthropólogicas. Lima, Peru, 1967.

Young, David, and Jean-Guy Goulet, eds. *Being Changed by Cross-Cultural Encounters. The Anthropology of Extraordinary Experience*. Peterborough, Ontario, Canada: Broadview Press, 1994.

SEPTRIONIC
BIBLIOGRAPHY

Shikry Gama. "La Fuerza del destino." n.d. 199. Unpublished manuscript.
———. "La Pobreza." n.d. 199. Unpublished manuscript.
———. "El Don e la Controlalidad." Unpublished manuscript, May 2, 1989.
Nathalie Lopez Zondervan de Cedaño. "Commentario, La Fuerza de Destino de Shikry Gama." N.p., n.d.

INDEX

Figure numbers reference the second color plate section.